# WHY I AM

## ☆ A ☆

# DEMOCRAT

BOOKS BY THEODORE C. SORENSEN

*Why I Am a Democrat* (1996)

*"Let the Word Go Forth"* (Editor) (1988)

*A Widening Atlantic? Domestic Change and
Foreign Policy* (Coauthor) (1986)

*A Different Kind of Presidency: A Proposal for
Breaking the Political Deadlock* (1984)

*Watchmen in the Night: Presidential
Accountability After Watergate* (1975)

*The Kennedy Legacy* (1969)

*Kennedy* (1965)

*Decision-Making in the White House* (1963)

# WHY I AM

## ☆ A ☆

# DEMOCRAT

## Theodore C. Sorensen

Henry Holt and Company
New York

Henry Holt and Company, Inc.
*Publishers since 1866*
115 West 18th Street
New York, New York 10011

Henry Holt® is a registered
trademark of Henry Holt and Company, Inc.

Library of Congress Cataloging-in-Publication Data
Sorensen, Theodore C.
Why I am a democrat / Theodore C. Sorensen. — 1st ed.
p.    cm.
Includes index.
1. Democratic Party (U.S.)    2. Republican Party (U.S.: 1854–   .)
I. Title.
JK2316.S63    1996                              96-10984
324.2736—dc20                                   CIP

ISBN 0-8050-4414-0

First Edition—1996

Designed by Betty Lew

Printed in the United States of America
All first editions are printed on acid-free paper. ∞

1   3   5   7   9   10   8   6   4   2

Dedicated to the Memory of
*Simon H. Rifkind (1901–1995)*
Faithful Friend, Partner, and Democrat

# ☆ CONTENTS ☆

# ☆ CHAPTER 1 ☆
## MAKING A CHOICE
☆ ☆ ☆

*I am a Democrat,* by conviction as well as affiliation, not by birth but by choice, not because of my parents or neighbors or spouse but because of my basic values and beliefs. I am not a New Democrat or an Old Democrat, a reconstructed or unreconstructed New Deal Democrat, a "different kind of Democrat" or a "yellow dog" Democrat, one who would vote the straight Democratic ticket even if the party nominated a yellow dog for office—and occasionally it has. I'm just a Democrat.

Some of my opinions on public-policy issues stamp me as a "liberal" Democrat, some as a "moderate," some as a "conservative," but for most of my opinions no single label makes sense. I receive no government or party payments of any kind, and no pressure from my law partners or clients, many of whom are Republicans. I am simply one of millions who find the Democratic Party's candidates, principles, and positions consistently preferable to those of the Republicans.

I do not claim that the Democratic Party has not had its share of demagogues, hypocrites, fools, and knaves. I do not claim that all its positions and programs have proved over time to be wise or workable. I claim only that among all the realistic choices before me, it is the best.

I do not speak for any party or public official, for any candidate or committee, for anyone other than myself. This book was not written at the request or with the endorsement of the Democratic Party. No one can speak for all Democrats. Our party has traditionally been characterized by more internal diversity and differences than the Republicans. That is sometimes our weakness but ultimately our strength. Democrats are by nature inclusive, not exclusive. We have long been and will long remain the country's most broad-based, multi-interest party, with a membership too independent-minded to be doctrinaire about everything and too undisciplined to be unanimous about anything.

Let me make it clear, then, that this book's references to Democrats, and their positions and party, describe the positions currently taken, as I see it, by most Democratic officeholders and party leaders most of the time. No doubt some passages describe how I hope most of them think, or how I believe most of them should think or once did think or will again think. So be it. My task is simply to explain why *I* am a Democrat. No one else may have the same explanation, or be interested in mine.

Similarly, my references herein to "Republican" positions describe those being taken by most Republican officeholders and party leaders today most of the time, as I see it. Some moderate-to-liberal Republicans may correctly complain that these sweeping generalizations do not represent their views. I am sorry about that. In fact, I am sorry for moderate-to-liberal Republicans. My father was one—once.

I do not condemn Democrats whose opinions differ sharply from mine, nor do I favor their expulsion from the party. Ideological as well as ethnic purification should be left to despots in other lands. Nor do I expect this book to change the course of newly Republican, formerly Democratic officeholders, particularly those in the South whose views are more compatible with current Republican thinking.

Have I ever voted for a Republican? Of course. "Sometimes," as John F. Kennedy said, "party asks too much." Have I ever been disappointed by the Democrats? Many times. I am disappointed now. I have also been disappointed on occasion in my country, my family, my law firm, my tennis partner, and myself, and I am sure that I have disappointed all of them on more than one occasion. But disappointment is not grounds for public denunciation or abandonment. My party affiliation is based on history more than personalities, on long-term principles more than pending proposals, and I am not willing to change that affiliation with every shift in the party's prospects, popularity, or leadership.

For any responsible voter with broad concerns, no single issue should be the litmus test of party support. But neither should a candidate's party affiliation (or even voting record) be sufficient reason to override serious questions about his or her character, judgment, or effectiveness.

Neither I nor any other American owes unswerving, unquestioning allegiance to any political party. Loyalty to its banner must be constantly earned and deserved. Nor should a political party become a business corporation directly serving the economic interests of those who control it, and held together by the patronage and payments it secures for its members.

I have never regarded myself as excessively partisan or ideological. But to vote is to choose—and one reason I am a Democrat in our two-party system is that I choose not to be a Republican. In making that choice, I measure my party not against some historical or theoretical standard of perfection but against the current Republican alternative. I would prefer in this book to uphold the Democrats in positive terms without mentioning the Republicans negatively (or at all), but it would be unrealistic of me to do so.

Nevertheless, unlike some Republican leaders I do not regard members of the opposing party as "grotesque," "abnormal," or "not American." Nor do I regard all their arguments as without merit or all their proposals as wrong. I would never go so far as the Republican pollster who found liberals to be the "least patriotic," the "most sloth-like" and "gluttonous," "untruthful," and "greediest" of all Americans in his objective poll, or even so far as the Republican senator who said that Republicans and Democrats come from different planets and employ different sides of the brain—nor even as far as John F. Kennedy, when he speculated to me one day in the Senate as to whether a visitor from Mars would be able to tell, merely by looking at his colleagues in session, which members were progressive and compassionate and which were hardhearted, stiff-necked Republicans.

I believe that both parties most of the time sincerely want what they deem best for our country. Public policy choices, I learned long ago, are rarely choices between good and evil, right and wrong, all and nothing, or between measures guaranteed to succeed versus those guaranteed to fail.

I do not believe that either of this country's two major political parties has a monopoly on truth, patriotism, or virtue. I served proudly in a Democratic administration that appointed Republicans to key cabinet and other positions. Both parties include scoundrels and weaklings within their ranks as well as dedicated public servants. Both parties cater excessively to big campaign contributors and local pork-barrel projects. Both have members who seek to impose their versions of "politically correct" conformity on the rest of the population.

Just as the long-ago Republican-turned-Independent mayor of New York, Fiorello La Guardia, said there was no Republican or Democratic way to collect garbage, so I believe there is not (or need not be) an exclusively Republican or Democratic way of fighting wars, floods, inflation, sleaze, the influx of illegal immigrants, narcotics, and terrorists or the waste of government money. Bipartisan approaches in Congress to foreign affairs are desirable whenever possible, and bipartisan coalitions in Congress are required to make most important and enduring domestic programs possible. A basket of legislative proposals, like a basket of fruit, must be judged on the quality of its contents, not its label.

Both parties are equally opposed, for example, to foreign nations closing their markets to American exports, to farm families being forced into foreclosure, to teenagers having babies or access to pornography, to our economy becoming excessively dependent on foreign oil, and to America's armed forces risking their lives in areas of marginal importance to our security. Both parties want America to be militarily strong, and both simultaneously vie for unwarranted military installations and weapons production facilities for their own congressional constituencies. Much of the time, the debate in Washington between the parties is over means, not ends; over distance, not direction; or, as House Speaker Newt Gingrich has said, over priorities, not substance.

But means and distance and priorities can be fundamental questions, often concealing in polite or technical language deeply felt differences over race, religion, money, power, or privacy. Appeals to bipartisanship should not paper over those differences that do make a difference—the difference between fair and unfair, equal and unequal, right and wrong. To cite some examples discussed in the pages that follow:

- Both parties today want to change the unsatisfactory status quo—but the Republicans, backed by lobbyists for various insurance, pharmaceutical, tobacco, gun, and other commercial interests, want to turn the clock back to pre–New Deal days, while the Democrats want to tackle the new challenges to job security created by trade and technology.
- Both parties, while denying it, seek a redistribution of wealth—the Democrats would direct a little of it from the richest 20 to 25 percent of our nation's population to all the rest, and the Republicans would direct it from the middle class and poor to the most affluent.
- Both parties want to drastically reform welfare with a healthy dose of "workfare," but only the Democrats are frank enough to acknowledge that this requires the availability of jobs, training, child care, and health care.
- Both parties seek to balance the federal budget over time by reducing the size and cost of government, but the Republicans' approach is far harsher than the Democrats' to the young, the ill, the elderly, and the least fortunate.
- Both parties denounce crime and violence on our streets, but only the Democrats target the underlying causes of that crime and violence and the guns with which so much of it is committed.

- Both parties purport to support health care and retirement security for senior citizens, but the Republicans would let "free market competition" largely determine access and adequacy, while the Democrats believe our elders deserve a guarantee.
- Both parties assert their opposition to intrusive and excessive government regulations and bureaucracy, but the Republicans would have the government intrude upon the privacy of a student's prayer and a woman's doctor, while reducing government safety inspections of the food and water we consume and the places where we work.

These differences are not minor details. They are basic differences, sharpened by the Republican Party's assault on government that followed its electoral victory in 1994, but obscured by Republican domination of the public debate in the months that followed.

I found the Republican congressional leaders' mastery of the 1995 legislative agenda depressing but politically impressive. So long as they succeeded in focusing that debate on numbers instead of values, in defining the principal issues as balancing the budget (while ignoring the imbalance in equity) and cutting taxes (while ignoring the consequent cuts in essential services), so long as they succeeded in claiming for themselves the high moral ground on issues to which the Democrats had a prior, equal, or even greater historical claim—concern for middle-class families, the spirit of patriotism and volunteerism, individual and community responsibility, combating crime, and maintaining a strong defense—they would succeed in having the game played on their turf by their rules to their advantage.

So long as they succeeded in asserting in simplistic but politically brilliant slogans a dubious voter mandate for irresponsible attacks on such essential government services as school lunches, student loans, Medicare, and environmental protection; so long as they succeeded in blaming the Democrats for the gigantic budget deficits and job insecurities that grew largely unattended during twelve years of Reagan-Bush rule; so long as they succeeded in wielding those deficits as a bar to government innovation and compassion—then the Democrats would be reduced to waging a losing defensive struggle over the scraps that remained under the government table.

I began to think about writing this book in early 1995, when a defeated, divided, dispirited Democratic Party abetted exactly that kind of Republican success. The crushing across-the-board rejection of the Democratic Party in the 1994 elections at every level and in every region appeared to have stunned many Democratic leaders and officeholders into temporary silence or inaction. Some briefly tried denial, unable to accept minority status. Others looked for someone to blame—for the defeat, for the lack of an effective counterattack, for the absence of a cohesive message. Congressional Democrats were accused of deserting their Democratic President under fire, the President was accused of deserting the Democratic constituent base, and the constituent base was accused of being a millstone around the party's neck.

Some congressional Democrats, uncertain how to be effective in their new role as members of the minority, fell into lassitude and depression. Some defected to the Republicans. A record number announced their retirement.

Disheartened, discouraged, and intimidated by attacks from well-organized and well-prepared Republican congressional leaders, conservative think tanks, and right-wing talk radio demagogues who falsely portrayed us as nothing but antibusiness, antiwhite, protax and prospending pseudo-Socialists, Democrats in Washington and elsewhere at first responded weakly or not at all, lying low or lying down. A mountain of myths and misinformation about everything ranging from United States law enforcement officers to United Nations peacekeepers, from the First Family's finances to welfare mothers' fertility rates, too often went uncontradicted and even unanswered.

Democratic answers, when they came, were frequently tentative or timid, lacking fire and conviction. Too often those responses looked wholly negative, political, tactical, lacking coherent, consistent themes or strategies and new ideas, with very few old ideas and very few constructive alternatives to Republican proposals. One public opinion poll after another said that most Americans, including most Democrats—even most Democratic members of Congress—were uncertain as to what the party or the President stood for, or what they should fight *for*, not just what and whom they should fight against.

Democrats rightly worried aloud about an identity crisis, a confidence crisis, an intellectual vacuum. Why was anyone a Democrat? A lost generation had never been given a clear view of any basic party objectives other than (1) winning the Cold War (now over), (2) helping minorities, cities, and the poor (now unfashionable), and (3) indefinitely controlling the Congress by dint of their traditional majority of Southern seats (now gone).

Prophecies of political doom can become self-fulfilling. In early 1995, with public opinion polls showing voter regard for the Democrats at an all-time low and with the prospects for their ever regaining a majority in the Senate or even the House looking dim and distant at best, there was much gloomy talk of the Democratic Party imploding, splitting into two or three or more factions, or gradually fading away like the Federalists and Whigs. (And that was just the Democrats talking!) One pundit wrote, "What this country needs is a second party."

In such an atmosphere, with more Americans turned off by both parties than turning out to vote, with increasing numbers identifying themselves in polls as "independent," "undecided," "don't know," or "none of the above," with voter registration in both major parties declining while Independent registration increased, it is not surprising that a few Democratic leaders and many Democratic voters were tempted by the siren song of a third party or Independent presidential candidacy. Many Democrats were attracted by the Colin Powell phenomenon—the man above both party and politics, belonging to neither left nor right, saying all the right things, reaching out to the tens of millions of nonvoters, a man who would somehow win the election and move the Congress without any organized support in that body. In the spring of 1995, pollsters announced that an absolute majority of voters, understandably frustrated and yearning for "something better," told pollsters they supported the launching of an Independent or third-party candidacy. The voters did not, however, promise to vote for such a candidate.

In modern politics, the Ross Perots, the John Andersons, the Strom Thurmonds, the Wallaces (Henry and George), and the other noteworthy Independent or third-party presidential contenders have usually been the voice of some disaffected regional, ideological, racial, or other faction whose views were not represented by either of the major parties. These candidates have been remarkably determined battlers for recognition. They have often been spokesmen for ideas previously rejected but later adopted, at least in part, by one of the two major parties.

But the one thing they have not been is winners. Unless there are extraordinary circumstances never yet present in this century and unless both major parties have nominated dunces, have neglected the middle of the political spectrum, or have utterly and continuously failed to address the important needs of a substantial portion of the electorate, it inevitably becomes clearer and clearer to the voters and financial contributors, as election day draws near, that—whatever the early hopes and hoopla—their favorite third-party or Independent candidate cannot surmount the political, legal, economic, and geographic hurdles that must be overcome to obtain a national popular or electoral vote majority in this country; that, instead, one of the two major party presidential candidates is going to win, however narrowly or undeservedly; and that one of those two major party candidates will be a better President than the other, however marginally. Under those circumstances, I have always deemed it an obligation of citizenship to cast my vote for that better major party candidate, however deeply disappointed I may have been in some of his positions or actions, and however skeptical I may have been about any likely improvement.

I understand why many people find voting for the lesser of two evils objectionable. But it is necessary to remind ourselves that voting for a third-ticket candidate with no reasonable prospects of victory can only help the "more evil" of the two major candidates become President.

Nor are the two presidential candidates ever equally "evil"—or equally "good." Any voter who reads or listens with care can discern important differences in their views and voting records, important differences in how they would behave in moments of crisis and in whom each would appoint to high office, important differences in how each would lead and would react to the failures and frustrations of leadership. In some election years, these differences may seem small and the choice unappealing. But a choice must be made.

Moreover, Independent candidates—with or without temporary, tailor-made third parties—who say they are "above" politics or who substitute personal piety and pleasing platitudes for hard decisions on controversial political issues are usually either naive or hypocritical and would almost certainly be doomed to failure in the Oval Office. Deadlocks and delays in Washington and the inadequate response to knotty problems like the decline in family economic security are not simply the result of failed personalities, waiting to be remedied by personal strength and charm. I do not want to be "rescued" from politics by a white knight unwilling or unable to balance a ticket, make a deal, form a coalition, compromise a policy, trade a favor, and displease a lot of people. Politics, with all its need for reform, is still the fiber of which democracy is woven, the grease that enables the wheels of government to turn, the cement that binds a diverse and disparate country. Most members of Congress will not long listen to a President who constitutionally lacks the legal authority to lead without them and politically lacks the practical tools to lead with them.

If an independent or third party candidate—or, worse yet, several of them—did in fact win enough states to block an electoral vote majority for either major party nominee, the President would be chosen by the House of Representatives on a one state, one vote basis, a surefire route to an undemocratic, bitterly divisive process that would leave the winner with a faint mandate and a fragmented nation.

There is still another option for disaffected voters: staying home on election day in order to send a message of protest. But that "message" is not distinguishable from those sent by 100 million others, most of whom are not protesting or disgusted or disillusioned but simply too busy or lazy, too ill informed or unconcerned, or too tired or far from home, to go to the polls. Disappointed protesters failing to vote only help the candidate whom they would most protest, while increasing within their own party the proportionate influence of those who disappointed them. In 1968, Democrats who stayed home to protest the tardiness of Hubert Humphrey's opposition to the war in Vietnam helped bring us Richard Nixon and five more years of intensified warfare (as well as Watergate, the lifetime appointment of conservative judges, and a great many other unfortunate consequences).

Despite that experience, there are always some disgruntled Democrats who prefer defeat in order to "teach the party a lesson" or who believe that only from the ashes of an electoral loss can a "purified" party be reconstructed to regain power. They deceive themselves. Only splinter parties can be ideologically pure. Defeat breeds defeat. While these purists are waiting for the Democratic Party to reconstruct itself in their image, a Republican President and Congress will be appointing Supreme Court and other federal judges for life, cementing their hold on voters and donors with the inherent advantages of incumbency, and finding it easier to inflict their policies upon less privileged Americans, who can look only to the Democratic Party for help. Exercising the privilege of neutrality at the expense of the underprivileged, among others, is not acceptable. The "lesson" for party leaders will be lost on them, and so will the hopes and causes that induced these now disgruntled Democrats to become Democrats in the first place. Those reluctant to seek a Democratic victory for the sake of the party should seek it for the sake of the country.

I respect those who prefer to register as Independents. My mother registered as an Independent. But as for me, I prefer to have a voice in the nomination process (a voice not given to nonparty registrants in many jurisdictions) and to state a choice between the two seriously contending parties. Party registration and affiliation increase political participation. It is tragic that in a democracy dependent upon the consent of the governed, relentless, cynically partisan attacks on government and politics have now undermined confidence and participation in the process itself.

That includes participation in political parties, now weaker and less influential than ever. Pollsters, professional consultants, and the media, both paid and unpaid, have largely replaced local parties as intermediaries between the candidate and the voter. Party leaders now control few votes, dispense still fewer jobs, and hand out no turkeys on Thanksgiving. They are accustomed to watching major candidates form their own separate election-year organizations and appeals. Even national party conventions are now rarely more than ceremonies ratifying the choice of candidates already made by the voters in state primaries and caucuses.

But our parties are still the custodians of our basic political principles. They still provide the continuity without which there would be confusion, the machinery and lists and expertise without which there would be chaos, the interconnected institutions that help provide a foundation or starting place for voter judgment and evaluation of candidates. Politics would be improved in this country if the nonfinancial roles and responsibilities of our two major parties could be strengthened in ways that would increase grassroots participation. The system cannot work if we do not participate.

A two-party system in a country as large and diverse as ours usually produces two coalition parties (one ranging from moderate to left and the other ranging from moderate to right), contesting for general-election votes in the middle of the spectrum and sometimes tugging the spectrum itself one way or the other. So long as both parties remain representative and viable, the system provides a reassuring degree of stability and continuity. I favor the two-party system. Even in these days of Democratic Party disarray and disappointment, I do not intend to support a third party. I do not intend to stay home. I am not an Independent. I am a Democrat.

In 1896, when the Democratic Convention nominated for President William Jennings Bryan, the Free Silver advocate and free-slinging orator from my native state of Nebraska, reporters asked the Democratic senator from my adopted state of New York, the more conservative David Hill, for his reaction to the nomination. He sourly replied, "I am a Democrat still—very still." Now, one hundred years later, when our party seems beset and beleaguered on all sides, when some party members keep silent in gloom or disgust, others are becoming Republicans, and still others look longingly at the possibilities of a third party or Independent presidential candidacy, I remain a Democrat still— and cannot remain still.

That is the genesis of this little book, short enough, I hope, to be read by those who run as they read (for office or otherwise), and long enough, I hope, to say more than the bumper stickers and fifteen-second commercials that inundate this season. The teachings of my parents, my schools, my church, and my principal political mentor and inspiration, John F. Kennedy, do not permit me to stay silent or complacent when values and principles and policies I hold dear are under brutal attack. This is one of those times when a great many of us need to reflect on whether we are Democrats. I have. I am.

Although I would not expect my personal conclusions to wholly coincide with those of any other Democrat, I hope that at least some of my conclusions can give comfort to Democrats who need it, ammunition to those who can use it, food for thought to those now deciding for themselves, and help to those trying to find their way through the fog of competing political claims and exaggerations. Although this work is not an autobiography, it is based upon a lifetime of political observations, mostly made as a private citizen. Although this work is not a history of the Democratic Party and is certainly not an apology for it, I cannot help but draw upon my own modest involvement in that party history. Although I support President Bill Clinton for reelection, this book is not a campaign screed for 1996—a crucial campaign year for Democrats, to be sure, but one certain to center on particular campaign issues and personalties that will rise and fall in the coming months with the tide of unforeseen events. I have in mind a longer perspective in writing about the oldest political party in the world, and hope this work will have relevance for many years to come.

For the same reason, I am not attempting here to write a Democratic Party platform, to stake out my position on every current issue or offer a solution to every current problem. My focus instead is on the basic, long-term principles and truths that have caused me to identify myself as a Democrat for many years past and that will, I trust, continue to do so for many years to come. It is those principles, I believe, not a laundry list of specific programs and prescriptions, that will determine the long-term survival and success of the Democratic Party.

Too many politicians (these days, especially Democrats), when asked what their party stands for, respond with a list of generalities that virtually *everyone* stands for. I intend to stress the principles that in my view distinguish the two major parties from each other.

My purpose is not to widen the gulf between the parties, for I recognize the need for compromise and comity in a democracy. Indeed, I deplore the tactics of confrontation, the resort to name-calling and bickering and the lack of civility that too often characterize the current contentious debate techniques of both parties. By chance, on the day this page was written, the press reported a single appearance in which Speaker Gingrich termed his adversaries and their positions "mindless," "obnoxious," "despicable," "weird," "disturbed," "dishonest," "irrational," and "absurd." All of us should remember that, as John F. Kennedy said in his Inaugural Address, "Civility is not a sign of weakness." Even in the most fractious congressional debate of his day, unlike today, comparisons of one's opponents to Nazis or Fascists were rarely heard and cries of "Shut up" were never heard. No one accused the President of treason or murder, or compared welfare recipients to animals.

Politics, I realize, "ain't beanbag." It is often rough and rarely dainty. But it is not a game or theater or academic contest. People's hopes and lives are at stake, the kind of society in which we live is at stake; and those entrusted with these decisions should treat them with the dignity they deserve. The ultimate object of political or legislative debate should be reconciliation and results, not polarization and stalemate. Democrats who practice reflex confrontation against anything proposed by the Republicans are making a political mistake. Republicans who engage in harsh, unfounded personal attacks on President and Mrs. Clinton violate the very biblical Scriptures they invoke in other contexts. Neither party deserves to win on the basis of voyeuristic tales of personal misconduct on the part of some member of the other party.

But Democratic Party civility and accommodation need not mean Democratic Party submissiveness or acquiescence. Harry Truman has been frequently quoted to the effect that voters confronted by a choice between Republicans and pseudo-Republicans will vote for the real thing. I agree. Democrats masquerading as a kinder, gentler version of Republicans lack credibility. Having served Kennedy when he was senator and President, I know that criticism of presidential compromises that bridge the divide between the parties on a particular piece of legislation comes more easily to legislators and candidates who would rather fight than enact. But it is also true that a party loses the election, loses its way, indeed, loses its very reason for being if it becomes merely a pale imitation of its opposition.

It is in this context that I have no hesitancy in setting forth what I perceive to be the fundamental long-term differences between Democrats and Republicans, differences that the bold Republican legislative program of 1995 has highlighted more clearly than ever. I have no hesitancy in urging my party to propose as well as oppose, if it is to continue to be the party of new ideas and not the party of the status quo. But reaching beyond the status quo does not require it to abandon its historic role as defender of the ordinary people who deserve our help and concern. Some Democratic programs may be stale, but our traditional principles are not.

I have no hesitancy, finally, in identifying—not urging or creating, but identifying—those clear, long-standing differences between the parties that some Democratic officeholders occupying shaky seats might prefer to blur or forget, on issues they might prefer to bury or avoid. Only if we make our convictions clear and act upon them will our party deserve to win, and win—and, even more important than winning, serve the "large and noble public purposes" that Woodrow Wilson said parties are created to serve.

In short, if the Democrats over the long run are to regain the confidence of the American people, merely to be against the Republicans will not be enough. To confine ourselves to defending old programs with new platitudes will not suffice. To rely on the skillful distribution of political spin and government spoils will not work. To run solely against the symbol of Newt Gingrich as for years we ran against Herbert Hoover will not do. To appeal primarily on the basis of class and classification—by appealing to groups on the basis of race, gender, religion, occupation, or geography—will not succeed.

I know all about those classifications. I was born to a Republican family in a Republican state. I was raised in a middle-class household. I make my living in the private sector, pay more taxes to Washington than I like, and am a champion of individual freedom and responsibility. I am an angry white male who has lived most of his life far from Washington, D.C.; as a lawyer I am committed to the rule of law and order in our society. I am a family man with a conservative life-style, I am an old-fashioned patriot, and I like to be on the winning side. Political scientists (an oxymoron?) would conclude from that description that I must be a rock-ribbed Republican. Most voters with most of those characteristics are Republicans, and most Republicans fit most of those characteristics. But, both despite and because of those very characteristics, I am a Democrat, and I am optimistic about the future of the Democratic Party. Let me tell you why.

## ☆ CHAPTER 2 ☆
### REMEMBERING THE PAST
☆ ☆ ☆

*I was a born to a Republican family in a Republican state.* In the year of my birth, the same year in which the Republicans won the presidency for the third consecutive time, my father was elected attorney general of Nebraska on the Republican ticket.

In 1928, a progressive reformer like my father had no difficulty finding a home in the Republican Party. It was in general a conservative party, to be sure, solidly led by Main Street businessmen, mainstream Protestant church patricians, free-market libertarians, and other respectable pillars of the establishment. They focused on the nation's economic development, and agreed with Calvin Coolidge that "the business of America is business." Although many of them would come literally to hate Franklin Roosevelt, they did not vilify the whole government or condone those who threatened violence against it. The legacy of Abraham Lincoln was as recent to them as that of Roosevelt is to modern-day Democrats, and many, perhaps most, believed in religious and racial "tolerance" and constitutional civil liberties to an extent that would have made them distinctly uncomfortable with the self-styled "revolutionaries" of the radical and religious right who dominate today's Republican Party.

The Republicans in those days had long included a progressive wing, particularly in many Western and Midwestern states. My father's close friend and political collaborator was Nebraska Senator George W. Norris, a Republican member of Congress since 1903, who thought liberalism was as "indispensable to life as the pure air all around," a progressive innovator who would later become the founding father of the Tennessee Valley Authority, the federal Rural Electrification Administration, and the statutory bar against antiunion injunctions. My father's political idol was Lincoln, the first Republican President, who established for all time the legal supremacy of the federal government and its moral responsibility to all Americans, regardless of color. My father's political inspiration came from another Republican reformer, President Theodore Roosevelt, who enhanced the federal government's power and responsibility to regulate the business trusts and their depredations of consumer and environmental interests, and who antagonized Southern racists with his appointments of blacks to federal positions and his invitation of Booker T. Washington to the White House.

Unfortunately, the policies of both Lincoln and T.R. were undone by Republican congressional majorities not too long after each departed the White House. Norris, increasingly isolated and under attack from his own party as he supported Franklin Roosevelt's measures for economic recovery and regulation, left the Republican camp to win reelection as an Independent in 1936 and then served as chairman of Independents for Roosevelt in the 1940 presidential campaign. His national cochairman was another disillusioned former Republican congressman, Mayor Fiorello La Guardia of New York. And his Nebraska state chairman was my father, who by then had hung a large portrait of F.D.R. in our living room.

By and large, that trend has continued to be the story of the Republican Party throughout my lifetime. The increasing isolation, repudiation, and intimidation of the moderate and progressive voices in the party confirmed for me my decision to be a Democrat. Republican Senator Arthur Vandenberg of Michigan would weep in his grave today if he could hear the verbal abuse heaped daily by the members of his party upon the United Nations, which he was instrumental in creating. The Capitol Hill statue of Republican Senator Robert Taft of Ohio, "Mr. Conservative," faces away from the wreckage being wreaked today by his party upon his cherished programs to help assure decent housing and a basic public school education for all Americans. Republican President Dwight Eisenhower's name is occasionally invoked by his party's leaders today, but not his persistent stands against those Republicans in his day who would have cut out the "safety net" programs of his two Democratic predecessors, trampled on the civil liberties of dissenting Americans, and solidified control over the Cold War budget by the "military-industrial complex."

The internationalism of 1940 Republican presidential nominee Wendell Wilkie and 1960 vice presidential nominee Henry Cabot Lodge—gone. The commitment in the sixties to civil rights of Republican presidential contenders George Romney and William Scranton—forgotten. Republican Vice President Nelson Rockefeller's provocative denunciation of extremists—erased.

Over the years many, perhaps most, Republican progressives left the party. Some, like Norris, La Guardia, former Senator Lowell Weicker of Connecticut, and former Congressman John

Anderson of Illinois, became Independents. Others, like former Senator Wayne Morse of Oregon and former Congressmen Don Reigle of Michigan, Leon Panetta of California, and John Lindsay of New York, became Democrats, as did several other members of the House. Not surprisingly, as Republicanism regained respectability in the South and Northern Democrats championed civil rights, Strom Thurmond of South Carolina, Phil Gramm of Texas, and other lukewarm Democratic officeholders switched to the Republicans, driving that party further to the right.

As Republican moderates have departed public office, their places have too often been taken by a new breed of hard-line, hard-right conservative. The few Republican moderates who remain today are a dwindling, hardy, but endangered species, frustrated by their lack of influence in their party and thus in public affairs, denying to the public and perhaps themselves that the party's leadership and proposals are or will remain so extreme, and in many cases embarrassed by their own silence and complicity. Their ranks still include some able, thoughtful legislators strongly opposed to their party's views on abortion, civil rights, and government-sponsored prayers in public schools, among other things. Frequently booed or heckled at their party's national gatherings if they dare to counsel moderation or even civility, the moderate Republicans have found their role consistently devalued by their conservative party leaders—except when their support is needed in the final stages of a floor vote or a presidential election campaign.

One of those conservative Republican leaders, Senate Majority Leader Robert Dole, personifies the rightward trend of his party. Once he favored affirmative action to help women and blacks, limitations on handguns and assault weapons, tax reforms to reduce the deficit, food programs for the disadvantaged, and even a hint of compassion for the hungry, the homeless, and those dying of AIDS. Not anymore. No doubt his rightward shift has been motivated by his quest for the 1996 presidential nomination of a party that shifted before he did, by his concern about the far right's increasing control of his party's convention and nominating process, and by his determination not to be outdemagogued by his competitors for the nomination. Last year these included men who started out to Senator Dole's right, like Pat Buchanan and Phil Gramm, as well as men who sought to rush in a rightward direction, like Governor Pete Wilson of California, himself a onetime sponsor of a widely applauded affirmative action program and of measures to increase immigration into this country, both of which he swiftly turned against when political expedience so dictated.

Senator Dole's increasing conservatism has reflected but did not lead his party's swing to the right over the last generation. Principal credit for that swing belongs instead to five others:

- Senator Barry Goldwater, who helped pave the way with his flat-out, no-holds-barred antigovernment campaign for President in 1964. Yet even Goldwater has decried the attempt of today's extreme right wing to "take the Republican Party away from the Republican Party."

- President Richard Nixon, whose administration provided much of the right wing's political underpinnings by his deft playing of the racial card in his so-called "Southern strategy" and "law and order" approach. Yet it was during Nixon's presidency that many of the pollution control, job safety, consumer protection, affirmative action, food entitlement, and other programs now under Republican assault were expanded.

- President Ronald Reagan, Goldwater's spiritual heir, whose simplistic "supply-side economics" sanctified ever-popular tax cuts in the face of enormous budget deficit increases.

- The Reverend Pat Robertson, never elected to public office but more powerful than most elected Republicans through his tightly organized and disciplined Christian Coalition, which has been quietly taking control of the Republican Party in dozens of states to advance its own religious-right agenda.

- Finally, Speaker of the House Newt Gingrich, who in a remarkably brief period skillfully if perhaps only temporarily pulled together all these elements: the silenced moderates, the uneasy old-fashioned fiscal and libertarian conservatives, the race-baiting conservatives, the supply-side conservatives, the religious conservatives, the anti-Washington conservatives, the purveyors of hate, anti-Semitism, and paranoid conspiracy theories, and the advocates of violence against law enforcement officers and abortion clinics. Speaker Gingrich and his highly disciplined House Republican majority welded all these disparate groups into a newly powerful political machine that pushed Republican senators and Republican presidential candidates further and further to the right. "Gingrichism," says former New York Governor Mario Cuomo, "is Reaganism with a scowl." The Republicans, I predict, will wish in time that they had denounced their far-right fringe in the way liberal Democrats fifty years ago denounced and excluded from their ranks American communists and their fronts.

The result is a Republican Party wholly unlike that in which my father served with George Norris—a party that, in sharp contrast with the Democrats, has become more aggressively homogenous in ideological, racial, and religious terms, more mean-spirited toward the poor, more nasty in its use of slash-and-burn political rhetoric, more rigid in its legislative positions, more negative toward government and those who serve in it, and more determined to regulate the morality of others but ignore free-market economic abuses. It is a party dominated by zealots and intolerant true believers who are not conservative, as that term was once understood, but self-styled "revolutionaries" of the radical right.

Meanwhile, the Democratic Party has undergone a very different kind of transformation from the big city– and Southern-dominated group that lost still another presidential election in the year of my birth. I was a child of the Great Depression. I remember asking my mother about the pitiful place we passed outside of town, where weather-beaten, wizened old men and women engaged in stoop labor in the sun. It was the county poor farm, she said, the only relief that local government could provide in those times. I remember the orphan asylum and the hobo camp and the tattered young men asking my mother at our doorstep if she had chores they could perform in exchange for food. I remember my uncle's farm, ravaged by drought, dust, and grasshoppers, without electricity and therefore without lights, running water, a refrigerator, radio, or other appliances. I remember learning, when I was old enough to pay attention to the radio and local newspapers, about bread lines and farm foreclosures and bankrupt businessmen jumping out of office buildings.

Then, in 1933 (though I claim no first-hand memories of this),

Franklin Delano Roosevelt, the new Democratic President and the founding father of today's Democratic Party, took office and took charge.

F.D.R. sought to put his stamp on Washington in his first hundred days in office. That historic effort, which in fact became known as the "Hundred Days," was invoked by the new Speaker of the House, Newt Gingrich, in January 1995. Mr. Gingrich having invited comparison of himself with the man he calls the greatest President of this century as well as of the respective initiatives they each launched during their first-hundred-day crusades, let me say simply this. The Gingrich Contract With America, reflecting the results of the Republican Party's public opinion polls and "focus groups," consisted largely of political symbols and procedural gimmicks that offered little or no direct alleviation of the problems faced every day by average American families. It was mostly negative and punitive: cut government services for the middle class and poor while cutting taxes for the rich, cut regulations on business, cut back U.S. participation in the United Nations, reduce the average person's access to judicial protection, repeal anticrime measures adopted the previous year, and limit the number of terms that members of Congress can serve.

By contrast, Roosevelt's "Hundred Days" in 1933 realistically addressed widespread economic distress and an entire nation's lack of business and consumer confidence and emphasized the positive: reopening the banks, developing the Tennessee Valley region, promoting the rights and opportunities of working people, putting young men to work for the Civilian Conservation Corps, feeding the hungry, protecting farmers, refinancing home mortgages, safeguarding small investors, and reorganizing the railroads, to cite only some examples.

In those "Hundred Days" of executive as well as legislative

action, wrote Walter Lippmann in that summer of 1933, a nation of "disorderly panic-stricken mobs and factions . . . became again an organized nation confident of our power to provide for our own security." In the months and years that followed, more plans and programs brought further hope and confidence, usually over the fierce opposition of the Republicans: Social Security, unemployment insurance, farm credit, guaranteed bank deposits, school lunches, regulation of stock market fraud and speculation, collective bargaining rights for organized labor, rural electrification, an end to child labor, minimum wages and maximum hours instead of sweatshops, protection for tenant farmers and sharecroppers and farm families, home loans for both farm and city dwellers, airline safety, fair employment practices for minority workers, and jobs and more jobs building schools and dams and bridges and parks and wilderness trails.

That is only part of the Roosevelt legacy, much of it forgotten by those who complain that government never works. Many of the children of families saved from destitution by the New Deal are today's contented conservatives. We have never seen anything like that era since. We have never again had a depression, in sharp contrast with the preceding century. We have never again had a senior-citizen poverty rate three times the rate of that for the general population. And, sad to say, never since that time have all those rights and safeguards been under such fierce attack as they are today. As Senator Daniel Patrick Moynihan of New York told his colleagues last year, "It is beyond belief that in the middle of the Great Depression in the 1930s we provided for children a minimum benefit to keep them alive, and in the middle of the successful 1990s, with a seven trillion dollar economy, we're going to take that away."

Of course, the New Deal is history, the story of a past that cannot be and should not be restored. But "what's past is prologue." A political party's history is one of its most distinguishing characteristics, one of the factors that a thoughtful citizen weighs in choosing between the parties on some basis other than a transient dislike of a particular candidate or ephemeral issue. Neither party can escape its history, primarily the history made by its former Presidents; and the Democrats have no reason to do so.

A century ago a caustic opponent compared the Democratic Party to "a mule—without pride of ancestry or hope of posterity." Wrong, then and now, particularly regarding our party's ancestry. Proud of our roots, which are part of the glue that holds our party together, we often invoke the past, beginning with Thomas Jefferson and Andrew Jackson, a history that spells out for more than two centuries the theme of activist Presidents in an activist federal government who built an America strong enough to protect the weak and vulnerable among us.

Ponder for a moment the line that has stretched, whatever its twists and turns, from F.D.R. to Clinton during my lifetime (which coincides with the lifetime of the modern Democratic Party), and compare that line with the line stretching from Herbert Hoover (elected in the year of my birth) to George Bush. Six Democratic Presidents: Franklin Roosevelt, Harry Truman, John F. Kennedy, Lyndon Johnson, Jimmy Carter, and Bill Clinton. Compare the record of the men on that roster, even acknowledging all their differences and imperfections and limitations, with the six Republican Presidents who served over that same time: Herbert Hoover, Dwight Eisenhower, Richard Nixon, Gerald Ford, Ronald Reagan, and George Bush. Consider the differences between those two rosters in terms of their visions and legacies for America, their concern for all, including ordinary and impoverished Americans, and their energy and activism in office.

No doubt, for those who prefer a passive, caretaker President, responsive primarily to those at the top of the economic pyramid, instead of an innovative, positive President who actively attacks the problems confronting the average American, the Republican six compare favorably with the six Democrats. But for the rest of us, I believe, the verdict is clear. The Democratic ethos, whatever its shortcomings, has been one of building and uniting. The Republican calculus has more often emphasized subtraction and division. One test of the presidential ethos is that suggested by Franklin Roosevelt himself: "not whether we add more to the abundance of those who have much . . . [but] whether we provide enough for those who have too little."

In recounting why I am a Democrat, I cannot refrain from describing more extensively one of those six Democratic Presidents—John F. Kennedy. I was a Democrat before my eleven years of service with him, and I would still be a Democrat today had I never served with him; but his impact upon my outlook and that of millions of others was deep and enduring.

He did not fit the stereotypical statistical profile of most Democrats. He was a white male New Englander, born to wealth, educated in politics by a truly reactionary father, and a fiscal conservative and Cold War supporter who never labeled himself a liberal or even considered himself ideological. But his instincts on public policy represented the very essence of a Democrat. He was, as he acknowledged, "an idealist without illusions." He detested injustice. He believed government could help. He brooked no intolerance, racial or religious. He cared about others. Having suffered from ill health and military combat, he strove to see that others did not. He loved politics. He admired public servants. He was an activist who wanted to act. He was a Democrat.

We often talked, especially in the pre-1960 years when the two of us traveled to all fifty states, about the mix of motivations that led some voters to be Democrats and some not. Raised a Catholic in Boston's school of ethnic politics, he was capable of expressing disdain for Irish Catholic Democrats in Ohio who, upon moving to the suburbs, became Republicans, and amazement that affluent Scandinavian Protestants in Wisconsin were Democrats. He enjoyed mingling with corn farmers and coal miners with whom he superficially had very little in common, and jousting with political bosses who were his reluctant supporters. He had a genuine respect and affection for many of his Republican as well as Democratic colleagues in the Senate and House, conservatives as well as liberals, especially those who showed political courage and integrity on tough issues; but he also had an acute sense of who in both parties was a political hypocrite, a coward, or the puppet of special interests.

His success lay in persuading Democrats North and South, black and white, liberal and conservative, rich and poor, to respond to his challenge of the New Frontier. Many, perhaps most, of the Southern Democrats antagonized by his civil rights legislation did not desert either him or the party, because they recognized that his health, education, regional development, food distribution, and trade programs helped their states and communities too. Liberal Democrats disappointed in his arms buildup and fiscal restraint did not sit on their hands, because they recognized that his improvements in housing, the minimum wage, and environmental and tax reforms were consistent with their objectives. Cynics who had doubted government's ability to accomplish anything opened their eyes at his successes in the space race, inflation prevention, the Peace Corps, the Nuclear Test Ban Treaty, and the peaceful resolution of the Cuban Missile Crisis.

He was not always successful. He was not always right. He was not flawless as a President or human being. But endless sensationalist allegations about his personal life or tragic death, his father or his friends, cannot diminish for me or countless others the remarkable and selfless contribution that he made to this country as a military officer, national legislator, and President.

It is difficult now, given the shortness of memory of most Americans regarding public events, for people to remember how his action-filled thousand days in the White House brought new hope all across this nation and beyond—hope that this country could live up to its full potential of excellence, hope for a world of peace and reason, hope that honest and effective government could right our nation's wrongs. I remember, and I remain, like John Kennedy, a Democrat.

I also remember our constant encounters with religious bigotry in his 1960 presidential campaign—the groundless charges that, under Kennedy, the beliefs of one religious faith (his) would be favored or imposed over others, that an officeholder's personal religious commitments (his) would interfere with public policy, and that the leaders of a particular religious organization (the Catholic church) would tell their congregations how to vote and tell their members who were elected officials how to act. It is ironic and chilling to note that the denominational heirs of those who made such false charges in the attempt to defeat Kennedy now engage on behalf of the Republican Party in the identical patterns and practices that they denounced with such vehemence and foreboding at that time: they now openly and expressly urge that their religious doctrines be favored over others, that their members in office set public policies according to those religious doctrines, and that their political views be binding on their congregations.

Not all religious conservatives opposed Kennedy then or are

Republican voters now. On the contrary, a substantial number of them supported him—working men and women who sought to better their situation in life; their jobs and retirement security; their access to health care, housing, and education for their families; the quality and safety of their communities and environment. These are the people who for many years were—and should be again—pillars of the Democratic Party.

Except on civil rights, Kennedy's fiscal and domestic initiatives were on the whole more moderate than those of his Democratic predecessors, Roosevelt and Truman, and Presidents Carter and Clinton have been on the whole more moderate than their Democratic predecessor, Lyndon Johnson. In part, this moderation was simply politically astute and practical, with the Democrats occupying the middle of the political spectrum as the Republicans moved further to the right. In part, Carter's and Clinton's political postures reflected the rightward drift of the nation itself, as it became fatter and more contented—largely as a result of Democratic policies—as bitter divisions over civil rights and Vietnam impaired Democratic unity and strength, and as both the memories and the scars of the Great Depression faded. Because of their moderation, Democrats in general, and liberal Democrats and union leaders in particular, have long been the target of harsh attacks from this country's small Marxist left: for their timidity with regard to economic reform and radical protest tactics and for their anticommunism at home and abroad, among other things.

But moderation has not spelled apathy or indifference. On the contrary, the Democratic Party's courageous commitment to the civil rights and equal opportunity of every citizen, its belief in the use of the federal government as a bulwark engine of economic growth and security, its protection of a woman's right to privacy and reproductive choice, and its loss of conservative voters and office holders in the South for reasons of race and otherwise, all while the Republican leadership moved sharply rightward, not only reduced the party's size but intensified the divisions between the two major parties in Washington, making the search for common ground more difficult. The resulting ideological, economic, and racial polarization in Congress, in Washington, and in our national political dialogue is not only disheartening but dangerous. Representative democracy was more adequately and less erratically served when *both* parties were loose coalitions of diverse philosophies, races, and factions, a profile that still describes the Democrats.

Today's ideological stratification is not only unhealthy but terminologically confusing. I am troubled by the extent to which I find myself relying in this book on such traditionally convenient but increasingly ill-defined shorthand words as "left," "right," "liberal," and "conservative." The "liberal" and "conservative" labels are both used (sometimes together!) by political parties all over the world that range from the truly democratic to the most repressive. Along with "left" and "right," they are usually applied in speeches by American politicians to other American politicians as meaning whatever nasty adjectives the speechwriter wants them to mean.

As the Republican Party becomes increasingly rigid ideologically, clustered on the Far Right edge of the spectrum, most Democrats, including myself, hold positions that could be deemed conservative on some issues, liberal on others, and pragmatic on most. But nearly all elected officials prefer not to be labeled at all, fearful that any description will offend some voters and mislead others.

There is no common "liberal" position on Bosnia or mandatory prison sentences, and no "conservative" consensus on farm subsidies or China. Neither capital punishment for juvenile offenders nor term limits for members of Congress will accomplish their backers' objectives, but is support for either of those measures "liberal" or "conservative"? If the status quo on federal regulatory standards is largely the handiwork of two generations of liberals, can defense of the status quo be defined as conservatism? (As far back as the 1952 presidential campaign, Democratic nominee Adlai Stevenson remarked in this context that American liberals had become the true conservatives of our time.)

If the new young Republican congressmen continue to call themselves "radicals" and "revolutionaries" out to dismantle the status quo with little regard for the consequences, are they still "conservatives"? Certainly some of them err in calling themselves "populists." The original Populists were squarely on the opposite side of the political divide between the impoverished and the elite.

When poll respondents say they want "smaller government" but more spending on education, health, safety, and all their other favorite programs and services, are they being conservative, liberal, or just unrealistic? Is a congressman who rejects more government intrusion into the sex lives of welfare mothers, gays, or abortion clinic patients an antigovernment "conservative"? Is one who rejects the request of the nation's police officers to get handguns, assault weapons, and "cop-killer" bullets off the streets of our cities a free-market conservative—even for criminals? Do Pat Buchanan's intemperate assaults on big business come from the "far left" or "far right"? In truth, most people no longer care about these labels.

Nevertheless, as broad generalizations characterizing one's philosophical approach to major ideological issues—such as the role of government—these terms are too useful as a discussion tool to be discarded completely; I aim in this book to use them carefully, consistently, and objectively as descriptive, not pejorative, terms.

Early in the 1988 presidential campaign, it was suggested on the Democratic side that the central issue of the Democratic campaign would be "competence, not ideology." In fact, that campaign was largely devoid of both. I reject the implication that there is no significant philosophical difference between the parties, no distinctive approaches to issues that matter to voters, only a difference in their respective governing skills. On the few but important issues where the terms "liberal" and "conservative" still have some meaning, more Republicans than Democrats more often think and vote "conservatively" and more Democrats than Republicans more often think and vote "liberally."

I resent and will not accept the endless Republican attempts to distort and demonize the word "liberal" as applied to the Democratic Party and others. I wrote in *The New York Times* after the Democratic election debacle of 1994:

> [If] liberalism is defined as its detractors would define it—as a simple-minded political philosophy that instinctively endorses reckless government spending, shameless personal conduct, toothless responses to crime and spineless foreign policy—then that philosophy has a barely perceptible pulse in American political life.
>
> But that has never been the true meaning of liberalism. A liberal mind is (or should be) the liberated mind—liberated from prejudice and hatred and cant, open to new ideas and solutions, neither permanently tethered to the dead hand of the past nor rigidly fet-

tered to any faction or fortune. . . . Authentic liberalism—the liberalism of Jefferson and Lincoln, Wilson and the two Roosevelts, Truman and Kennedy— lives on.

Democrats fearful that the Republican campaign to redefine "liberal" has irreversibly succeeded in tilting public opinion against the term will sometimes use other labels, such as "progressive" (another term with a grand political history—except in 1948—that to many of us is interchangeable with "liberal"). For self-styled "liberals" and self-styled "progressives" in the Democratic Party to fight one another is not only foolish but self-defeating. The Progressive movement in the first quarter of this century was championed by both Republicans and Democrats, but that heritage has now been wholly abandoned and forgotten by the Republicans.

I care very little for labels. I care about contents. The contents of the new Republican Congress's plan not to improve or modify but to fully dismantle the economic achievements and safeguards of the last two generations, without regard to what is essential, what works well, what has served our nation best, what our people need, and what will take the place of these safeguards is not "liberal," "progressive," "moderate," or even "conservative." It is radical in the extreme, irresponsible, punitive, unjust, and dangerous. It is bad for the country. Only the Democratic Party can overturn it. I am proud that I am a Democrat.

# ☆ CHAPTER 3 ☆
## SECURING ECONOMIC JUSTICE
☆ ☆ ☆

*I was raised in a middle-class household in a middle-class neighbor*hood in Lincoln, Nebraska. My parents were never very rich nor very poor. I am fortunate to have now earned enough in the private sector to be economically comfortable, to have sufficient assets, income, and education to make it highly unlikely that my family will ever fall into poverty. Most voters with that economic background are presumed to identify, out of self-interest, with the Republican Party; and the Republican Party has attempted to portray itself as the party of the middle class as well as the rich, labeling the Democratic Party as the party that speaks only for the poor.

In fact, the Democrats have traditionally represented the interests of the middle class and those aspiring to enter the middle class and need not surrender that franchise now. In fact, Republican policies today are abetting economic trends that are making not only the rich richer and the poor poorer but the middle class smaller and more vulnerable, as more families slide into poverty. In fact, current Republican policies, if not altered, could well lead in time to a different kind of America, in which a small number of very rich live behind gates and guards, a large number of very poor have no stake in a cohesive and orderly society, and middle-class Americans—their security in every sense shrinking along with their numbers—become an endangered species trapped, perhaps for life, in between.

That is not an America I would want for my children and grandchildren. In many of the countries to which I have traveled on business or otherwise, I have seen ugly disparities of wealth and income—not only the luxury hotel surrounded by squalor but also the educated business and government elite controlling a country's economy and politics from well-protected offices and hilltop homes, traveling through dingy and dangerous streets with armed personnel. Despite free-market economic policies, virtually every one of these class-stratified countries has been inherently weak, divided, and unstable, unable to push back the encroachment of slums and poverty. I do not wish to see America moving in that direction.

Nor do I wish to be alarmist. The sky is not falling—yet. We are still the richest country on earth, with the most productive workers on earth, and with jobs, national income, and productivity still rising. We have become neither a resource-rich but impoverished Zaire nor an economically stratified Britain.

Instead, we have become a *more* economically stratified society than Britain. Indeed, we have become the industrialized democracy with the most unequal distribution of wealth and income on earth. President Kennedy often observed that economic growth served every American's interests because "a rising tide lifts all the boats." For more than twenty-five years after World War Two that was true. Not anymore.

For more than two decades, the median for the real wages and benefits of middle-class workers in this country has been stagnating or declining. Increases have not kept up with the cost of living, even when inflation has been under control. Young families, workers without college degrees, even those with college degrees but without advanced graduate school degrees, to say nothing of those who are unskilled or high school dropouts, have been losing ground. Many who have lost their old jobs have been unable to find new ones, or have been required to accept new jobs at substantially less pay. Many have fallen out of the middle class, or have avoided doing so only by straining to work longer hours, or by working two (or more) jobs simultaneously, or by requiring both parents of small children to work outside the home, or by compelling an older child to go to work instead of school.

When I was growing up in that middle-class neighborhood in Lincoln, Nebraska, the implicit American promise was economic progress for all—a job for everyone willing to work hard, at least a middle-class living standard for everyone graduating from high school, a share in productivity gains for everyone helping to achieve those gains, and the best standard of living and most egalitarian society of any country on earth. None of that can be promised any longer. The American Dream, the tradition that each generation of middle-class American workers would earn more and live better than their parents, has come to an end for tens of millions. Despite working longer and harder than ever before, despite a rising national productivity and income to which their labor contributes, those workers' real wages have fallen, in many cases below the poverty line, and their share of the national income has been reduced.

Political pundits report that the members of the middle class are angry. Of course they are angry. The average fifty-year-old worker has not seen a real raise in twenty years. One third of the young men aged twenty-five to thirty-four cannot earn enough to keep a family of four out of poverty. They feel insecure, with good reason, about their jobs, health insurance, retirement, and purchasing power. They have been denied their proportionate share of the national wealth and income that they have helped to create over the last twenty years. Republican politicians have directed this anger toward the poor, the people on welfare getting handouts. But the poor are not getting the middle class's share of the enlargement of the national pie. On the contrary, in America the poor themselves have become still poorer, more numerous, more desperate. Their children—and *one out of every five* American children lives in poverty—are worse off than any children in the industrialized world, and more likely than ever to remain poor for life. Their parents' paltry incomes are shrinking, and the chances for those children to get out of poverty through good schools and good jobs are bleak at best.

What united the middle class and poor under the banner of the Democratic Party ever since the advent of F.D.R. was this country's unique tradition of upward economic mobility in an expanding economy, giving every poor American child a chance to become a middle-class American adult, and every middle-class American adult the prospect of a secure and healthy old age. But America no longer leads the world in economic and social mobility; those without college degrees or certain technological skills are more likely to move downward, from the upper-middle-class family of their birth to the lower middle class, and from working poor to very poor. The only Americans consistently doing better over these last two decades have been those at the top: the top 20 percent, the top 5 percent, especially the top 1 percent, who control as much wealth as the lower 40 percent.

In a diverse free-market economy, some disparity in wealth and income is both inevitable and desirable. Incentives and individualism are important to progress. But the gap between rich and poor in this country is now greater than it has been at any time since the start of the Great Depression in 1929, greater than in any of the industrialized free-market countries of Western Europe and Canada—and growing.

Democrats have no wish to turn millionaires into paupers. Indeed, they do not object to the rich getting richer, particularly when their creative talents, energetic efforts, and sound investments enlarge the national pie for everyone to share. My father's friend, Republican Senator George Norris, said in 1929. "I make no complaint against wealth as such. I have no condemnation against the man who honestly acquires a vast fortune. It is the misuse of wealth that deserves our condemnation." What Democrats dislike is the rich getting richer at the expense of everyone else, particularly those whose labor is helping to enlarge the pie but who receive a smaller piece in return.

Republicans, after first denying these worrisome facts about worsening economic inequality in America, now proclaim instead its acceptability. They argue that the poor are always with us; that the free market both produces and is stimulated by inequality; and that the Republican Party, the party of the affluent and influential, will continue to succeed as long as most Americans believe, despite growing evidence to the contrary, in their own chances to move up to that top notch. If middle-class workers are suffering, blame it on the poor, the blacks, the immigrants, and the Democrats.

The Republicans are right in part—America stands for equal rights and opportunities for all, not equal results or equal assets. But what happens if those trends continue to accelerate and worsen, as a result of Republican policies? Increasing economic inequality, lagging wages, and a lower standard of living for much of the younger generation form an explosive combination in a free society. "An imbalance between rich and poor," wrote Plutarch almost two thousand years ago, "is the oldest and most fatal ailment of all republics." Not any imbalance, surely. But how much longer can these trends continue, how much wider can the gap between rich and poor grow, before our economy, our domestic tranquillity, the very fabric of our democratic society suffer the consequences?

When average workers read that the boss is now receiving a paycheck 150 or more times the size of theirs, and that their extended efforts (at the expense of leisure or family time) have helped increase the company's profits while their own real wages and benefits have fallen behind the cost of living once again; when they find that their chances of moving up in life to anything remotely approaching the boss's standard of living are present in theory but unattainable in fact, and that their children's chances of moving up even to their own standard of living, if they cannot afford college, are even dimmer; when they confront the fact that even this "pedaling in place" is no insurance against layoff in a fluid job market—then how much longer will they have the "team spirit" and sense of "empowerment" that modern M.B.A.s now emphasize are necessary for a workforce to be competitive?

Those insecure workers whose share of the pie is shrinking are the consumers our economy needs to purchase our products. Those children who are being brought up in poverty, with all the attendant consequences on their education, health, and attitude, are this country's future labor force, expected to compete with citizens of other countries raised in less dire circumstances.

The middle class and poor constitute the great bulk of our citizenry. They are the people who populate our streets, man our machines, serve on our juries, and vote in our elections. If their health, education, and family life suffer from these economic strains, then every rich American's risks increase.

If those who are left out, left behind, and left too little for their families to get by on resort to drugs or violence or crime, if their sense of desperation breeds contempt for a society in which they no longer have a vested interest, contempt for its laws and institutions, and in time contempt for human life itself, then the sense of community and common purpose essential to capitalism, democracy, and political and social stability are gone.

Lincoln said this nation could not long survive half slave and half free. I do not believe that America as we know it can long survive half poor and half rich, in an indefinite state of affairs in which the rich get still richer, the poor get still poorer, and the security of those in between gets weaker and weaker.

"Are there no prisons?" asked the miserly Ebenezer Scrooge in Dickens's *A Christmas Carol*. "Are there no workhouses?" And Speaker Gingrich echoes, "Are there no orphanages?" Of course there are. But the cost of building those institutions and maintaining their inmates is far greater than the cost of feeding, educating, training, and employing the least privileged of our fellow Americans. Right-wing pundits like to warn of the dangers to moral fiber and independence that come from "rewarding need."

Rewarding? By providing the desperately hungry child at most $1.06 per meal in food stamps, I suppose we take away his initiative to obtain food in some other way—say, by begging, stealing, or scavenging.

I do not place all blame for these long-term economic trends on the Republican Party, although they were accelerated during the twelve years of Reagan-Bush rule. As Washington wiseman Ted van Dyk has noted, the combination of Reagan's tax cuts for the wealthy and payroll tax increases for working families made him "a reverse Robin Hood, taking from the poor and middle class and giving to the rich." Economists ascribe the origin of these trends primarily to the rise of technology in the postindustrialization "Third Wave" Age of Information, to the rise of global competition for trade and investment, to the consequent shift in this country from manufacturing to services, and to all the corporate restructuring, relocating, automating, and downsizing that has resulted, putting middle managers, professionals, and white-collar workers as well as unskilled laborers out of work.

But I do fault current Republican congressional leaders for their callous indifference toward these long-term developments and those suffering from them, for their own tax and policy measures that can only worsen these developments, and above all for their rejection and destruction of Democratic programs designed to moderate these trends through public investments in education, job training, employment, and other initiatives whose purpose has been to provide poor and middle class alike with an opportunity to improve their lot. Democrats do not believe it is the federal government's responsibility to make all Americans equally rich or equally poor, but they do believe that government policies must not aggravate excessive disparities. Most of the world's industrialized countries in recent years have struggled to cope with similar long-term trends. But only the United States is doing so by punishing its unskilled, uneducated, and unemployed.

The only sure way for most Americans to climb the "ladder of opportunity" in the new economic era forged by expanded trade and technology, with its shortages of highly skilled workers and unskilled jobs, is through improved education and job training. That helps workers, their companies, and their country, assuring more employment, more competitive skills, more productivity, and more earning capability, as well as helping to curb these uncomfortably large wealth and income gaps.

- The *Head Start* program, whatever its errors in expanding hastily, has helped millions of preschool children develop the learning habits that will serve them well throughout life.
- Various forms of *federal aid to education*—to facilitate the development and application of basic standards, to assist school districts serving poor populations, to assure safe and drug-free classrooms, and to improve curricula in accordance with changes in our economy—have been of enormous benefit to countless children entering school for the first time and to countless adults returning to school for the last time. Yet today's Republicans savaged all of these programs at their first opportunity.

Indeed, they sought to divert funds from the limited resources available to our public schools into a voucher program assisting the more exclusive private schools and academies that some parents have chosen to establish. *Privately* funded voucher programs have proved to be a worthwhile experiment in many communities, and parent-student choice among *public* schools deserves exploration. But as a parent and grandparent of children taught in public schools, in private schools, and at home, I can think of no justification why our public schools, free and open to all but consistently handicapped by a lack of sufficient funds, should be still further penalized in this fashion.

- To go out into the job market without a higher-education diploma today is statistically comparable to looking for a job during the Great Depression. The lack of a college education is a greater handicap in today's economy than ever before in our history. But college tuition is also more expensive than ever before in our history. A substantial majority of young Americans today find higher education, like health care, priced beyond their reach. The *student loan* program, streamlined by the Clinton Administration to reduce both costs and abuse, is literally a lifeline for millions of young people whose parents' income is too low for them to afford higher education for all their children but too high to qualify them for grants from most colleges. Yet the Republicans cut back this program and increased its costs to students. Incredible. "Cutting education in the Information Age," said Senator Edward Kennedy, "is like cutting defense at the height of the Cold War."
- Many of those students unable to go on to college, and particularly those who drop out of high school, will end up on welfare, on the street, or in jail if they are not subsequently taught skills now in demand. America can-

not continue to be the only industrialized nation without
a vocational apprenticeship program.

• Work experience is gained, and our local areas are
served, by federal programs that find summer jobs for
idle youths and virtually unpaid *community service jobs*
(Americorps) for idealistic volunteers.

• Job training and retraining programs, both public and
private, are indispensable in an era when trade and technology bring rapid change to the job market, and these
programs need constant reexamination and retooling. A
worthy Democratic proposal would make it possible for
each unemployed or low-paid worker to select which
two-year community college or other training program
best suits his or her needs. But all of these programs—
including job training, vocational assistance, summer
jobs, Americorps, even the *Job Corps* (a particularly cost-
effective program), have been blocked or cut back by the
Republicans.

The Americans who struggle hardest to make ends meet, who
are denied full-time jobs or well-paid jobs or are forced to work
as "independent contractors" without health or pension benefits
or for poverty-level wages, those who are struggling not to be a
burden to others, not to be dependent on welfare, who are on the
wrong side of this country's growing wealth and wage gap but
deserve better—in short, the "working poor"—have become a
particular target of new Republican policies. House Minority
Leader Richard Gephardt has said, "Democrats think low wages
are a problem. Republicans think low wages are a solution."

The real value of the federal *minimum wage* has declined by
more than 30 percent to its second lowest level in more than forty

years. Contrary to Republican assertions that minimum-wage recipients are all youngsters or immigrants, most of them are adult
American citizens, many of them trying to support their families,
buy food, pay the rent, and pay their medical bills on today's
minimum wage of $4.25 an hour. Try it. Yet the Republicans
oppose any reasonable increase.

Continuing an ideological mind-set going back to their initial
opposition to Social Security and Medicare (lest we forget), the
Republicans also oppose comprehensive *medical insurance* that
could not be snatched away when a worker who may be only one
uninsured serious illness or injury away from poverty loses his
job or changes employers. They opposed the *Family Leave Act,*
which enables a worker to take time at home to care for a new
baby or dying parent without risking his or her job. They oppose
inexpensive quality *child care* for the children of working mothers, the *earned-income tax credit, affordable housing* for low-paid
workers, and the ability of *trade unions* to protect their members.
They urge reliance instead on the free-market principles of
"trickle down" economics, but for two decades very little has
trickled down from those at the top.

These Democratic programs are not handouts to the shiftless.
They offer a hand up to those who work hard but earn little.
Republican Senator Phil Gramm of Texas, in justifying why tax
cuts should go primarily to the wealthy, said he had "never been
offered a job by a poor person." No doubt. He has never been off
the public payroll in the course of his entire career. But I repeat: it
is the labor performed by poor as well as middle-class persons
that makes possible this nation's productivity and wealth, including its job opportunities—even the payment of senators' salaries.

To call attention to this grim picture is not to engage in "class
warfare," as the Republicans so often charge. A party that seeks to

cut taxes and regulations for the economically secure, while simultaneously eviscerating the safety net beneath the economically insecure and in effect raising taxes on the poor, is surely in no position to accuse others of class warfare.

In 1995, the Republican Party declared war not on poverty but on the poor as never before. Its new measures devastated the working poor, as already described, along with other working families, and then crushed even more thoroughly those without work. Acting apparently on the theory that the rich will work harder if given more breaks and the poor will work harder if given fewer breaks, the Republican zealots cut back every poor family's prospects for getting food stamps, school breakfasts and lunches, nutrition support for poor pregnant women and infants, and the Medicaid program on which millions of ill and disabled depend, most of them children.

Ignoring the negative impact of national policies on trade, technology, education, housing, drug inflow, and urban development on our poor and low-skilled population, and ignoring numerous studies showing that most poor people are working or seeking work, often holding two jobs simultaneously because of the low and declining size of the average welfare check, the Republican leadership castigated the poor for being poor, called them loafers and deadbeats for not getting jobs or better-paying jobs, and blamed young mothers for not rushing back out into the labor market. Above all, they condemned and sought to basically scrap the collection of now politically unpopular programs, rooted in Roosevelt's battles against economic depression, known as welfare. For the first time in sixty years, they declared proudly, there was to be no American commitment, no assured safety net offered, to every American child at risk.

True, after sixty years, no one really liked welfare any longer, not even its proponents, administrators, or recipients. Politically it was regarded as a loser: even Democrats always received more votes and more support from the middle class than from the poor, especially the nonworking poor, most of whom do not vote. They could have and should have (but had not) reformed welfare themselves long before the Republicans wrecked it; but in 1995 no congressional Democrat wanted to continue unchanged a program that had for too long encouraged among too many a cycle of dependency, an almost impenetrable bureaucracy, and the dehumanization and humiliation of the program's own beneficiaries.

But neither did any fair-minded Democrat want to join in utterly destroying a sixty-year-old fail-safe system (as the Republicans in effect sought to do)—particularly without some replacement. For all its faults and failures, it had helped millions of very young children and their mothers weather a dismal period of typically three years or less until they could get back on their feet, helped low-wage earners obtain the health- and child-care and other services that enabled them to work, helped untold numbers of widowed, divorced, and deserted women through a cashless transition to a better life, helped reduce this country's tragically high rate of infant mortality, and helped countless children of poverty obtain the education and work experience they needed to leave the slums behind. The national commitment that made those life-saving, democracy-enriching achievements possible cannot be simply kicked away without an alternative. "Ending welfare in this country as we know it" might be easy, if only ending poverty as we know it were not so hard. It speaks volumes that the principal first-year boast of the new Republican majority was its legislation pushing poor children deeper into poverty and malnutrition and widening the industrialized world's largest gap between rich and poor while continuing to provide tax cuts and subsidies for the affluent.

Despite much middle-class antagonism toward welfare, the economic prospects of the poor and the middle class in this country tend to rise and fall together. My middle-class neighborhood in Lincoln, Nebraska, could not have survived the 1930s if New Deal assistance had not helped far less secure neighborhoods reduce the incidence of poverty, disease, and ignorance among their children. The common interest in economic advancement that is shared by the poor family deprived of hope and the middle-class family deprived of opportunity should link them together politically under the Democratic banner, not pit them against each other as the Republicans seek. The Democratic Party has no political need to abandon its representation of either the poor or the middle class. The downfall of Prime Minister Margaret Thatcher's right wing rule in Great Britain has been attributed in part to her mean-spirited treatment of the poor, which not only belied the moral pretensions of her party's "capitalist revolution" but also undermined her own political standing. That is a hopeful precedent.

President Kennedy in his inaugural address said, "If a free society cannot help the many who are poor, it cannot save the few who are rich." Democrats can and will help the many who are poor in this country with the same emphasis on education, training, health, and opportunity with which they must help middle-class workers regain their purchasing power. This is not a time for further economic disparity and class stratification in America, for cutting programs that aid the middle class and poor twice as deeply as all other programs, or for denying to working

Americans their fair share of the additional wealth they help to create. It is not a time for "trickle down" economics. It is a time to strengthen our economy from the bottom up, on a basis of equity and justice, in a spirit of fairness and hope.

That approach ultimately helps and protects us all. It is both the democratic approach and the Democratic approach—an important reason why I am a Democrat.

# ☆ CHAPTER 4 ☆
## UTILIZING OUR GOVERNMENT
☆ ☆ ☆

*I make my living in the private sector.* Like my father before me, I have spent most of my adult years in the private practice of law, representing primarily corporate clients, often advising them about foolish, confusing, or outmoded government regulations. During my fewer than thirteen years in government (1951–1964), I saw first hand the kind of ineptitude, indifference, and inertia that antagonize so many citizens. As a close observer of government over the years, I have frequently deplored the gross manifestations of its chicanery, cupidity, and stupidity, from the Bay of Pigs to the Iran-*contra* affair, from Watergate to Waco.

In that context, if the Democratic Party had in fact become the "party of government," as its critics allege, instead of the "party of the people," as its history attests; if its leaders were in fact addicted to the invocation of federal government intervention as the first, last, and only solution to any and every problem; if every Democratic leader's knee-jerk response to every new question or crisis were to propose a new government law, program, agency, or appropriation; if, as Republicans allege, to be a Democrat means believing that the government is always right, always wise, never wasteful or incompetent or ineffective, then I could no longer be a Democrat. Indeed, I would not wish even to reside in the country described by many Republicans in which all Americans are dependent upon the tolerance and beneficence of an omnipotent, omnipresent government that ignores the public's needs and wishes, a government generally out of touch and out of control.

Fortunately, that kind of heavy-handed paternalism does not remotely reflect the views or wishes of the Democratic Party, nor does it remotely resemble the state of the Union under any administration, past or present, Democratic or Republican. Democrats believe in better, not necessarily bigger, government, in making a more energetic and effective use of government within the limited resources and jurisdiction granted to it by the people. We look upon government in appropriate situations as a useful instrument of our common purpose as a people, not as an end in itself. Like Thomas Jefferson, we view government skeptically as a threat to liberty as well as liberty's protector. Like Woodrow Wilson, we believe government should serve society, not manage it, and that most of the time its power is best used not to coerce but to catalyze, coordinate, stimulate, guide, or, under certain circumstances, compete.

We recognize that there are many tasks that government cannot perform well, including the selection of favored industries to be subsidized and the prescription of moral conduct; unlike the Republicans, we have steadfastly opposed unwarranted government interference with freedom of expression and intrusive government meddling with individual rights of privacy and prayer.

We want government to promote liberty, not stifle it. We believe in utilizing government to expand opportunity, not in utilizing every opportunity to expand government.

Democrats, unlike Republicans, recognize the value, particularly in difficult or challenging times, of affirmative, activist government. We have held that belief at least since Franklin Roosevelt, in the depths of the Depression, paralyzed in body but not in spirit, "conceived of the federal government as the whole people organized to do what had to be done" (in the words of one of his advisers). Republican Theodore Roosevelt had said much the same thing even earlier and simpler: "The government is us; we are the government, you and I."

The government, Democrats believe, is a written reflection of the unwritten social contract, the acceptance by all citizens of the reciprocal obligations to society that accompany their obligations to one another as individuals. This includes the obligation to govern themselves through formal public bodies on matters where self-discipline and self-regulation (through the family, the market, and other private means) will not suffice. When government is honest, efficient, and democratically representative of the people's will—constant effort is required to make it so—we believe it can be an indispensable means by which society can improve itself, curb the inevitable ills, excesses, and injustices of the private sector, and improve the human condition and sense of community for all.

Unlike average citizens, those who have wealth and power rarely need government to protect them from exploitation or neglect. But they still need government—to facilitate national and international trade and transportation; to maintain law and order; to promote science, the arts, and education; to fight pollution, recession, and inflation; and to stimulate economic growth and consumption. Those who are weak and vulnerable—because they are too young or too old, too poor or too gullible, too unorganized, too inarticulate, too subject to discrimination or disaster—need government most of all: as a friend and protector to safeguard their right to justice and liberty and to help them up the ladder of economic opportunity.

Although it has become politically fashionable in recent years to bash all government programs as incompetent and ineffective, I am one of countless Democrats who look back with pride on the accomplishments of F.D.R.'s New Deal, Truman's Fair Deal, J.F.K.'s New Frontier, and Johnson's Great Society. Those programs included errors, excesses, and misjudgments, but they were not failures. On the contrary, they rebuilt and reshaped this country in myriad ways: dramatically reducing poverty and illness among the elderly, infant mortality among the poor, fatal accidents in the workplace, and hazardous waste in our waterways, to name but a few. We know government can work. It can help.

The Republican view of government, in contrast, tends to be wholly negative—cramped, pinched, pessimistic. In Republican eyes government should be a clerk, not a leader, playing a passive role, not an active one, except for its unanimously accepted role in maintaining public safety and national security, guarding our lives, borders, and property against physical harm. Glossing over both the history and the reality of modern America, today's Republicans seek to turn the clock back by eviscerating the federal government's ability to grapple with our economic, social, and other problems.

They believe that the best answer to every problem is to reduce the size and effort of the federal government. They have yet to explain how crime will be reduced in our streets, or how our goods will become more competitive in world markets, or why our middle-class citizens will feel more secure about their jobs, pensions, medical costs, and children's college tuition, if federal programs addressing those issues are decimated. Indeed, Republicans readily believe that government *is* the problem, in Ronald Reagan's words, and never part of the solution, that government has caused our major ills and never solved one.

Of course, Republican congressmen, while condemning the role of government in respect to the less privileged, have no objection to the federal government's participation in research, export promotion, and other subsidies handed out by Washington to numerous industries and corporations. And Republican governors, while supporting much less federal money for those who are hungry, handicapped, or unemployed through no fault of their own, have no hesitation in asking Washington for large sums of federal money to help their states' industries and homeowners when they are buffeted by floods, hurricanes, or other natural disasters through no fault of their own. And Republican Presidents, who controlled the federal executive branch for twenty of the last twenty-seven years, made no significant effort actually to roll back the size, cost, and reach of the federal bureaucracy that they had so vigorously condemned when out of power, and in fact extended the federal reach in many areas, such as environmental protection and business subsidies.

Nevertheless, at least in principle, the Republican Party has traditionally preferred a weak federal government under a weak chief executive, a government in which private interests take priority over the public interest, conflicting local interests take priority over the national interest, presidential power is subordinated to—not even equal to—congressional power, the fiscal cost of government is of more concern than the human cost of injustice, and social problems like unemployment, stagnant wages, poverty, and discrimination are regarded as inevitable, unsolvable, or both.

Given the tendency of so many Republican politicians to invoke the Founding Fathers and their "original intent," it is noteworthy that they accept government's responsibility to secure the rights of life and liberty but not the pursuit of happiness, the opportunity for all Americans to improve their lives and living standards, their health and knowledge, their access to the wonders of art and nature. Government cannot assure, much less deliver, happiness for all Americans. But there is much it can do and has done to help give ordinary citizens the same opportunity to pursue happiness as the most fortunate among us. Republicans don't think so. Democrats do.

The Republican philosophy was summed up in an uncompromising manner by House Majority Leader Dick Armey: "The market is rational and the government is dumb." Fortunately, the government is not always dumb—legislation on Social Security, school lunches, the G.I. Bill of Rights, and clean water, to name but a few, was not dumb. Furthermore, the market is not always rational—particularly when dominated by speculation, manipulation, panic, or greed.

Our nation would be ill advised to depend wholly on either the government or the market to make all national decisions and solve all national problems. Democrats favor leaving to the market those problems that the market can handle better and more cheaply without loss of fairness and accountability. We believe in providing the market, if necessary, with additional incentives, standards, and regulations that will enable it to better handle those problems. We believe in utilizing the market, when appropriate, as supplier, partner, or agent. We recognize the market, not the government, as necessarily the chief economic engine in a free society. But we do not believe that markets, any more than governments, are always wise, trustworthy, or efficient. Certainly they are not always fair and equitable, in either purpose or result, and matters of public concern cannot always be left in private hands.

On the contrary, markets by definition are founded on self-absorption and self-interest (usually spelled G-R-E-E-D). That is as it should be in a free, competitive, and incentive-based economic system. Public policy, in contrast, must involve considerations of conscience, community, and responsibility to others. Markets are designed to produce differences, not equality, in an environment where the only survivors are the economically fittest, not necessarily the wisest, kindest, or most creative. The market's "invisible hand," as posited by Adam Smith, makes wheels turn and steamships steam, but sometimes that hand is a clenched fist that knocks many people down and some people out. Governments are needed to tame these excesses, to temper their consequences, and to protect investors, consumers, workers, and others from such market distortions as monopoly, manipulation, discrimination, and exploitation.

Republicans say that the public sector is inefficient and wasteful compared to the private. Having worked in both sectors somewhat longer than many of the young Republican congressmen now making this argument, I would not give either sector a perfect score. Government expenditures are more subject than corporate expenditures to red tape, most of it imposed by Congress. Private-sector expenditures are more subject than public expenditures to executive whim, such as private jets and executive dining rooms. Government hiring is distorted by patronage, corporate hiring by nepotism.

Government too often has the hubris that comes with monopoly. But not all free enterprise is competitive, and not all competition is healthy. Unrestrained nationwide economic competition in the 1920s brought about the market manipulation and economic hardship that required government correction in the 1930s; unrestrained worldwide economic competition as well as domestic merger mania in the 1980s has likewise resulted in excesses and hardships requiring regulatory and protective government action in the 1990s.

A ruthless, unrestrained free market, with none of the restraints provided or encouraged by government—and thus driven only by profits—can produce shoddy goods, fraudulent securities, quack medicines, and illicit narcotics. It can also produce the pornographic and violence-oriented movies and recordings that the Republicans are quick to denounce. Senator Bob Dole accused Hollywood of "putting profit ahead of common decency." That is exactly what F.D.R. could have said sixty-three years ago about those operating sweatshops or employing child labor. It is exactly what Democrats could say today about those paying subminimum wages or promoting racial discrimination or union-busting tactics. Such a market may be "free," even "rational," in terms of commercial interests, but it is not acceptable in a society that cares about values as well as profits.

The choice is not simply between the government and the market. In real life the two are often blended. Government in this country depends largely upon its contracts with the market to supply its necessities (including arms), to buy and sell its bonds, and to implement most of its programs. The market depends upon the government to provide even-handed and expert regulation, as well as financial and other forms of help in developing new products and new overseas sales opportunities. There is no industrialized democracy on earth today that is free from the economic and human strains imposed by the global competition and technological advance discussed in the previous chapter. None of those countries, even while emphasizing privatization, pursue a wholly laissez-faire approach toward either their competitive posture in world markets or the widening wealth and income gaps afflicting their populations.

This blending and tempering of the American free market for the benefit of the American people does not seem to have done the market much harm. Since the earliest New Deal days, the U.S. gross national product per person, adjusted for inflation, has substantially multiplied in size. Many specific successes in the marketplace have been due to government research, assistance, or protection. Most of my Republican clients and friends, even while grumbling about bureaucratic bumbling, acknowledge that long-term business success depends upon strong public institutions fairly enforcing fair and specific rules, and upon all participants in the market, buyers as well as sellers, employees as well as employers, having confidence that the market will work reliably and equitably for all of them—which would be impossible without government watchdogs. Incidentally, many of those friends and clients, while voting Republican, also acknowledge that their businesses have generally prospered under Democratic administrations.

When I was growing up in Nebraska, the private electric companies made a "rational market decision" not to extend their power lines at substantial cost over great distances into lightly populated rural areas. The Rural Electrification Administration, championed by Roosevelt, Norris, and my father, was born of necessity. These power lines having now been built, Nebraska's and America's farm families having now long enjoyed the blessings of electricity and purchased appliances accordingly, the Republicans want the R.E.A. demolished or privatized. Perhaps. Privatization, deregulation, and the shrinking of government's role in the market have proceeded over the last two decades, where appropriate, under both Democratic and Republican administrations. But where it has not been appropriate, where the size or nature of a government activity made it impossible for the private sector to profitably, and therefore competently, take over a public responsibility in accordance with public objectives, the consequences of privatization—where public policy considerations and public accountability requirements confront private business leaders with a very different set of challenges than those of the dollar-and-cents bottom line to which they are accustomed—deregulation or "leaving the problem to the free market" has often been disastrous.

For example: under President Reagan, the savings and loan industry was freed from "burdensome and restrictive" regulations; the fraud and bankruptcies that resulted cost the taxpayers more than $150 billion. To make way for the private sector, federal assistance was deeply slashed for low-cost housing, the fight against poverty, and care of the mentally handicapped. The result was a stark and tragic growth in the number of homeless people begging and sleeping in our cities' streets and doorways. Human values and hopes are not as easily traded, sold, or discounted as commercial products and services. I well remember Robert A. Taft's comment on the corporate executive cabinet assembled by President Eisenhower: "I'm not at all sure that all these businessmen are going to work out. I don't know any reason why success in business should mean success in public service." Amen.

We can expect more disasters from the latest Republican efforts to turn back the clock—for example, on environmental protection and medical coverage for the elderly, disabled, and poor. I do not believe for one moment that the American electorate in the Republican congressional sweep of 1994 mandated the resulting congressional assault on the funding and scope of those programs. Bureaucratic failures should be slashed. But these were successes.

Federal environmental protection programs in 1995, many of them initiated or strengthened under Republican Presidents, represented not failure overall but success. More waters had been made fishable, swimmable, and drinkable and had been protected against the plundering of polluters and developers. More forests, wildlife areas, ecosystems, and species had been preserved in the interests of our nation's biological diversity. More air had been made more breathable and less visible. More roadsides and toxic waste dumps had been cleaned up. The purpose was not merely to enhance the quality of life but to protect the very viability of life on this planet. Much, much more remained to be done, but, far from continuing this work, the congressional Republicans reversed it, cutting inspection and protection programs from the Florida wetlands to Alaska's woodlands.

It saddens me to predict that in time we will all notice the difference, our children most of all, as a result of the Republican surrender to lobbyists for oil refiners, chemical manufacturers, loggers, and other industries bent on reversing the greening trends of the last twenty-five years. Of course, Republican legislators were not totally blind to considerations of ecology. Last October an advisory memorandum from the House Republican Conference, referring to criticisms from "the Environmentalist Lobby and their extremist friends in the eco-terrorist underworld," urged Republican Congressmen to improve their image by planting trees and handing out seedlings. (I am not making this up.)

Both Medicare for our senior citizens and Medicaid for our less affluent citizens had long enjoyed similar public support. Medicare kept its patient population from falling prey to irreversible poverty as the result of illness. Medicaid kept its patient population from falling prey to irreversible illness as the result of poverty. Both programs assured the children of those patients that they would not be required to exhaust their own, often limited household budgets to provide that protection for their parents.

There was agreement in both parties that the substantial costs of both programs had risen steeply (though no more so than private insurance) and had to be moderated, that benefits for higher-income recipients could be limited, and that an end to overcharging, fraud, and similar abuses was overdue. But congressional Republicans, in order to save enough in outlays to make possible their tax cuts for the well-to-do (not "to preserve and protect" these systems as repeatedly alleged), wanted to go much further: to cut far more funds from the future growth of these programs than keeping them out of insolvency required, ensuring over time steep increases in costs and reductions of benefits or coverage, and inducing beneficiaries to go back to the private insurance companies, whose previous unwillingness to cover, for example, preexisting conditions or postretirement ailments had necessitated these programs in the first place. (In fact, "saving" Medicare from its alleged bankruptcy should never have been entrusted to either the Republican Party or the health insurance industry, who together fought Medicare's creation at a time when half our older citizens were unable to obtain *any* health insurance.) As a substantial portion of the federal budget, Social

Security, Medicare, and Medicaid no doubt exemplify "big government." But they also exemplify necessary government.

The Republican decision in 1995 to go far beyond the necessary modernization and modification of existing domestic programs and to undertake instead their destruction was not limited to environmental protection and health care. I thought protecting the lives and safety of citizens had been presumed to be a universally accepted responsibility of government. No, said the Republicans, not worker safety in the nation's factories, mills, and mines, where federal standards over the past generation have sharply cut the number of deaths and injuries from falls, fires, faulty equipment, and foul air. And not safety for American consumers, who without sufficient government inspectors and regulations will unknowingly eat tainted meat, fish, and poultry, or take dangerous toxic medications.

Of course, those promulgating new regulations on health, safety, or the environment should be mindful of the costs to taxpayers and property owners. But they must also be mindful of the cost to an unprotected public if effective regulation is undermined or abandoned. In fact, many of the Republican regulatory "reforms" would require new, detailed cost-benefit, risk-return analyses, and compensation to adversely affected property owners, which will in turn require more paperwork, more bureaucrats, and the expenditure of more federal money. The answer to regulations that are duplicative, one-sided, wrong-headed, excessive, or unjustifiably expensive is better rules, not an absence of rules.

At least since the New Deal, most voters have consistently told pollsters that they would prefer smaller, balanced federal budgets financed by lower taxes. Who wouldn't? They particularly want less spending on welfare and foreign aid, two programs that they incorrectly assume represent a significant part of the budget. But most voters are equally consistent in the apparent inconsistency of telling the same pollsters—and Washington—that they do not want any reductions in federally financed services that benefit them directly. In fact, rich and poor alike, regardless of race, region, occupation, or gender, have continued to ask both parties to enact additional programs and provide more benefits. Nor do they seek the emasculation of government as an instrument of common policy. They want to see it work better, not disappear; to address, not dodge, our major national problems.

But having listened for decades to politicians assailing one another and the "bureaucracy" on grounds of dishonesty and ineffectiveness, and having repeatedly observed deception and incompetence in high places, the voters are also understandably skeptical. If the Democratic Party is to preach with any success the utility of government as a problem solver, then the party had better make certain that any government it runs is as effective, responsive, and lean as possible.

In fact, the number of civilians in the federal executive branch, nearly half of whom work for defense and defense-related agencies, is smaller than most people think. Contrary to widespread assumption, that "bureaucracy" has been steadily shrinking as a proportion of total population and employment for half a century. Federal spending has increased during this period primarily because of checks mailed out under Social Security and Medicare, not because of a growing bureaucracy. In recent years the bureaucracy has shrunk in absolute as well as relative terms. The Clinton administration's "reinventing government" effort has contributed to this shrinkage, eliminating, for example, hundreds of dubious advisory committees and dozens of local Department of Agriculture offices (reflecting the long-term decline in our rural population). Every modern President, regardless of party, has taken office with a vow—and often with a blue ribbon commission—to reinvent, restructure, reevaluate, reengineer, or otherwise reexamine the size and structure of the federal executive branch, and some have even usefully done so.

But sometimes it is dangerous to receive what we wish for. The reduction of an arbitrary number of federal personnel or government departments is not necessarily a boon to good government. Leaving an underpaid, understaffed, and underappreciated team of administrators in a particular department without experienced managers, inspectors, lawyers, and accountants is an invitation to both error and fraud. Overreliance on private corporate contractors, whose employees are not as thoroughly screened or scrutinized, has frequently led to conflicts of interest, kickbacks, and other scandals or to highly publicized overpayments.

Change for the sake of change in the structure of government sometimes costs as much in terms of disruption, lowered morale, and moving expense as it saves, particularly if the functions and services provided by the abolished agency, bureau, or department are ultimately transferred to some other box on a reshuffled organization chart. Nor should anyone be under the illusion that the abolition of cabinet-level agencies, any more than their creation, actually solves any *substantive* problem. Princeton professor of government John J. DiIulio, Jr., noted: "Abolishing the Department of Education will not improve test scores."

Unlike a number of Republican presidential candidates, I have not spent my career on the public payroll. But I am a former public servant and proud of it. I have continually urged young people to enter public service, on either a short-term or long-term basis, as a means of helping others and giving something back to society. During my four all-too-brief years in the executive branch, one year at a very low level and, nine years later, three at a very high level, I found most of my colleagues at every level to be able and dedicated men and women. I found the executive branch to be more productive and efficient in its use of public funds than the legislative branch, in which I served for over eight years, and I also found it better able to attract topnotch talent than most state and local governments.

In my international travels then and since, I have found the U.S. bureaucracy relatively smaller and more responsive and our citizenry more efficiently governed and less heavily taxed than those of any other country in the world. I have frequently observed from close range other democratic or would-be democratic free-market–oriented governments whose lack of sufficient public funds, public-servant expertise, and discretionary executive power led to economic instability, corruption, and private-sector ripoffs. As the president of the Twentieth Century Fund, Richard Leone, has written, "Countries with weak public sectors are more commonly known by another term—underdeveloped countries."

I realize that vast improvements can still be made in Washington, and the Democratic Party must not be complacent on that front. Incompetent government employees and anachronistic government programs and rules need to be weeded out constantly on an individual basis. I am sympathetic with everyone who has ever waited for hours to see an unsympathetic agent of the Internal Revenue Service or the passport office, or filled out ridiculously redundant forms—mostly aimed at preventing the very corruption about which we complain. Too many unread reports, most of them required by Congress, are still ground out every year. Too many administrators have too many administrative assistants, executive assistants, deputy assistants, and confidential assistants to the deputy assistant. Too many of them, in both Democratic and Republican administrations, participate in what conservative savant William Kristol has rightly criticized as "the Iron Triangle of the welfare state—the politicians, bureaucrats, and interest groups who establish and benefit from its programs"—a description equally applicable to nonwelfare bureaucracies.

But most of the federal employees I have known are hardworking, committed to their country's service but often capable of earning far larger salaries under far less stress in the private sector. Their daily successes receive no media coverage and little thanks, and their daily tasks are mostly taken for granted. But they keep our country going. When we need them to serve us, save us, protect us, rescue us, help us, or defend us, they are there. They work for us.

That is why it offends me to hear Republicans like Pat Buchanan label Washington bureaucrats "nice people, but . . . not that bright"; to hear Speaker Gingrich warn that the federal bureaucracy is a "threat to the nation"; to hear practically every Republican candidate for Congress and the presidency over the last thirty years, with the admirable exception of George Bush, run on a platform denouncing the federal executive branch and all who staff it as inept and untrustworthy.

What I have not heard from their lips is any repudiation of the right-wing talk-show hosts who say America is "held captive" by its government and that federal law enforcement officers engaged in their duties should be shot in the head. I have not heard them repudiate the bizarre government conspiracy theories of the Reverend Pat Robertson, founder of the Christian Coalition. In many a Republican heart there still abides, I fear, the spirit of Wisconsin senator Joe McCarthy, the xenophobic zealot who some thirty-five years ago advanced his career solely on the basis of ruthless and almost entirely unfounded accusations and exaggerations about supposed Communists in the federal government and finally became too much of an embarrassment even to his own party.

American politics, historian Richard Hofstadter noted during McCarthy's heyday, has long included a "paranoid strain" going back at least to the Know-Nothings of the middle of the last century, another anti-immigrant party. That strain is most evident today in the private armed militias in many states, who train in the backwoods in preparation to shoot any federal agent who tries to seize their guns, lands, or churches as part of these militias' bizarre notions of some United Nations, feminist, gay, or Black Power plot. Republican leaders, while enjoying the fruits of their own campaign to build public contempt for federal bureaucrats, deny any connection with these militant fanatics, whatever goals and fears they may share. This is disingenuous: in the volatile, suspicious climate of today, the venomous Republican and talk-radio rhetoric about federal employees turns mistrust into anger and anger into hatred, encouraging the view that the federal government itself is an evil and alien enemy tyranny whose laws should not be accepted and whose law-enforcement agents need not be respected. For those with gullible, troubled, or twisted minds, that way lies a future with more Oklahoma City Federal Building bombings.

Firebomb a synagogue or black church yesterday, an abortion clinic today, a federal building tomorrow. Too many loyal and innocent U.S. government employees have been shot, assaulted, or taken hostage, while doing their duty at home as well as abroad, for me to regard last year's Oklahoma City outrage as an isolated incident unrelated to the right-wing poison in the atmosphere.

The columnist Mark Shields has observed that Republican orators urgently in need of a villain to replace the defunct Soviet Union have now substituted the "fed scare" for the "red scare." How illogical and unwarranted is this "constant bashing of government," said Senator Bob Kerrey, from my home state, this "relentless assumption that forces beyond our control run our government . . . that we are victims of our own government. What nonsense! This government is ours!"

It is ours. To improve it, strengthen it, and enhance its management, all of us regardless of party should be thanking and encouraging our career servants, not demeaning them. We should be acting to keep the government lean but not crippled. We should be remembering government's role over sixty years ago in saving capitalism from its own excesses, and looking to government once again to ease the hardships and to moderate the extremes accompanying our latest transition into a new economic era.

There have been times in our nation's history when strong federal leadership has been essential, as exemplified by the presidency of Franklin Roosevelt. There have been times when a pause for consolidation and digestion has been appropriate, as exemplified by the presidency of Dwight Eisenhower. Today, with the post–Cold War world in a state of transitional disorder politically and America's leadership and each individual American's security under challenge economically, the next decade is no time for passivity in Washington.

The Democratic Party, more committed than the Republicans to the use of government as an agent of economic change, is consequently better at the art of governing, especially during such times of change, and more committed to moving our nation forward and reducing the pain that accompanies economic transition. Republicans may be better at tearing down and rolling back—but this is not the time for a negative approach. There may someday be periods in the life of this country when all its citizens enjoy such nearly universal prosperity, equity, and tranquillity that an active federal government is not necessary. This is not such a time. This is a time for more, not less, public investment, public education, and public employment.

The Democratic Party, out of power in the federal executive branch for twenty of the last twenty-seven years, cannot accurately or fairly be called the "party of government." Nor should it become such a party. But a fundamental issue distinguishing Democrats from their opposing party remains their belief in the utilization of an ably staffed and innovatively led federal government actively meeting whatever large-scale problems and crises confront this country. From my position in the private sector, I welcome that kind of government leadership. That's another reason why I am a Democrat.

# ☆ CHAPTER 5 ☆
## DIVIDING THE PIE
☆ ☆ ☆

*I pay more taxes to Washington than I like.* I realize that "taxes are what we pay for a civilized society," as Oliver Wendell Holmes said long ago, but not all of my taxes go to advance civilization. Like everyone else, I am appalled by the high cost and waste of government. Having had some responsibility for each of President Kennedy's annual budgets, I recall with pride that he alone among the post-Hoover Presidents never permitted a deficit as high as $10 billion. Though he governed at the height of the Cold War arms race, he never submitted a budget reaching $100 billion. Even taking into account inflation, expansion, and essential new programs over the last thirty-three years, I see no justification for the current long string of deficits exceeding $100 billion each, particularly in prosperous years, and no excuse for annual budgets of well over $1.5 trillion.

Kennedy's self-imposed ceilings on the budget and deficit required him to make tough choices among meritorious programs—that, he believed, was his job. He did not believe that many problems could be solved by merely "throwing taxpayers' dollars" at them, or that all our problems would be worsened if fewer tax dollars were spent on them.

Today, I am aghast every time I read that interest charges alone are three times as high as Kennedy's total budget. That single outlay is squeezing out the funding of necessary and constructive initiatives. More important, those excessive government deficits and expenditures, by draining funds from the private savings pool available for investment, are inhibiting our economic growth and productivity, dimming our hopes for ending wage stagnation, and unfairly shifting our burden to generations yet to come.

Does this make me consider "turning" Republican? Not for one minute. The Republicans may preach more loudly the virtues of fiscal austerity, but their past practices give them little or no credibility on this issue with me or millions of others. It is the height of hypocrisy for Republican Party leaders, in order to justify their slashes in health, housing, and education for the middle class, elderly, and poor, to point with apparent horror and alarm at the staggering national debt that was largely amassed by their own party's actions during the twelve years of Reagan-Bush rule.

Promulgating massive income tax cuts at a time of huge military budget increases, Reagan, with his "supply-side economics" (or "voodoo economics," as George Bush called it before embracing the idea to the tune of his own $255 billion deficit), inflicted on the nation annual budget deficits that cumulatively tripled the national debt that it had taken all of Reagan's thirty-nine predecessors two hundred years to amass. Presidents Reagan and Bush not only made this nation the world's largest debtor, but also, by causing our debt, now over $5 trillion, to increase much faster than the national economy, were forced to borrow enormous sums from foreign sources, which in turn helped to saddle us with an endless stream of devastating trade deficits. The bigger his budget deficits became, the more President Reagan borrowed at home and abroad to cover the difference and the higher the additional annual interest payments became in Washington.

This spend-more-tax-less "free lunch theory of government," said former Republican Senator Lowell Weicker of Connecticut, makes any Democratic spendthrifts "look like minor-leaguers." Even Senator Dole stated in 1982 that Reagan's policies were ignoring reality, but by then the train had left the station. True, congressional Democrats shared the blame for approving those budgets, but let it be noted that the Democrats consistently reduced the amount of imbalance in the budgets submitted to them. The single most important legacy from the Reagan-Bush era for our current national economy is the staggering national debt overhanging us all, a debt that continues to grow each year—though, let it again be noted, at a much reduced pace under President Clinton.

Even forgetting for a moment the Republicans' primary responsibility for the current state of fiscal affairs—and apparently they do forget, or why else would they still believe that cutting taxes even further in the face of these deficits will on balance increase revenues—their newfound crusade to make balanced budgets the overarching issue of our time seems less a genuine conversion on the evils of deficits than an excuse to cut off federal help to those who need it:

- No political party truly committed to the primacy of a balanced budget would have promised a $250 billion tax cut until that balance had been actually achieved, not merely promised.

- No political party sincere in its opposition to the national debt would be so reluctant to reduce, much less eliminate, what is rightly termed "corporate welfare": generous but unwarranted tax loopholes benefiting high-income corporations and individuals; research grants and incentive payments; free federal facilities and services to business; insurance and loan guarantees; concessions and natural resource giveaways; commodity, export, and transportation subsidies; and all the other payments, preferences, and "entitlements" given to sizable and successful companies and industries that can do perfectly well without these handouts. These subsidies cost the taxpayers each year far more than a combination of all the children's hunger, health, and related programs that these same generous Republicans have so extensively curbed.

- No political party honestly intent on eliminating the deficit would have forced on the post–Cold War Department of Defense, whose budget already exceeds those of all other NATO members plus Russia and Japan and all potential enemies combined, tens of billions of dollars for weapons that the department will not need, could not afford, and did not want. Will the security of the average American over the next seven years be more enhanced by keeping Medicare, Medicaid, student loans, school lunches, food stamps, and job training programs at full strength, or by forcing upon the Pentagon, over its objections, twenty more B-2 bombers for $16 billion, another Seawolf submarine for $2.4 billion, and a revived and revised missile defense system (né "Star Wars") that will eventually cost, as noted by Democratic Senator Byron Dorgan, "forty billion dollars on a project we don't need, with money we don't have"?

- No political party genuinely dedicated to zero budget deficits would have been so tolerant of expensive pork-barrel projects, local public works projects not approved on their merits but inserted into the budget by scores of Republican congressmen and senators (John McCain of Arizona being a notable exception) for the sole benefit of local constituencies and campaign contributors.

- No party sincerely devoted to fiscal prudence would have threatened repeatedly in the fall and winter of 1995–96 to refuse a legislative increase in the statutory debt limit, as blackmail to force through its tax and budget cuts. Such a refusal would have pushed the United States government for the first time into default on its Treasury bills and bonds around the world, inevitably bringing higher interest rates to all American borrowers—especially the U.S. government itself, to the tune of hundreds of millions of dollars. (Fortunately, that threat was never carried out.)

But all these corporate subsidies, tax loopholes, redundant weapons, and pork-barrel projects have added substantially to our national deficit without relieving any of the American people's fundamental problems. The shameful irony of it all! While federal aid to independently wealthy corporations continues, federal aid to dependent children is slashed—as if the 1 percent of federal spending that goes to the 2 percent of Americans on welfare were a significant cause of the deficit. While subsidies for giant companies studying experimental forms of heating fuel are renewed, subsidies to help poor citizens obtain heating fuel are abandoned. While millions of dollars are paid to corporations to educate foreign countries about their products, millions of dollars are cut from Head Start programs to educate American preschool children (even though this country already badly trails its competitors on the percentage of total government expenditures devoted to education). While entitlements are preserved for promoting the exports of powerful agribusiness companies, entitlements are eliminated for the powerless poor on welfare. While instances of "waste, fraud, and abuse" in health and nutrition programs are cited to justify their virtual elimination, the presence in military procurement programs of much worse waste, fraud, and abuse is conveniently overlooked in justifying the programs' expansion. While subsidies to large corporate farms continue to guarantee up to $250,000 per farm resident, funds for mother and child nutrition are cut back to the bone.

For members of the labor force who are unemployed, underemployed, underpaid, or simply insecure, and for families lacking assured access to medical care, safe neighborhoods, and a college education for their children, the question of whether the annual federal budget deficit will be reduced to zero by the year 2002 (the year agreed upon in negotiations between the congressional Republicans and the Democratic administration) or two years later or five years later is not the overwhelming issue of our time. Why should it be? In relative terms, this country had a far greater debt burden during World War Two, a burden that was heavy but did not sink us or prevent us from making vital investments in our people, for example, the G.I. Bill of Rights. Instead, that deficit was reduced gradually as the economy grew, without starving either the federal benefits programs that helped to stimu-

late consumer demand or federal education and training programs that advanced our productivity. In fact, it was the
economic growth facilitated by just those programs that both
reduced the relative impact of the debt burden and produced
more tax revenues to reduce the deficit. Yet Republican legislators
have slashed their modern counterparts.

The fiscal policies of the postwar period meant that in 1979,
before the Reagan spend-and-borrow philosophy took over, both
our deficit and our budget as a percentage of gross domestic
product were small compared to those of most advanced economies in the world. Even though those numbers shot up under
Presidents Reagan and Bush, today the relative debt burden for
the United States is still smaller relative to our gross domestic
product and relative to other industrialized countries than at any
time since 1979, for the economy has grown steadily and the
annual deficit has shrunk steadily during the Clinton administration. In fact, were it not for the enormous interest payments due
on the debt incurred during the Reagan-Bush years, there would
be no budget deficit at all this year.

Moreover, the average citizen trying to understand why the
Republicans are insisting upon an absolute zero deficit in five
years has good reason to suspect the integrity of both their vow
and their numbers. Reaching their goal even on paper depends
on highly speculative assumptions and projections: on future
Congresses' resisting pressure to tinker with hundreds of controversial pledges to which they are not bound; on arbitrarily not
counting large but emergency or other urgently needed appropri-
ations that are "off the books"; on predictions that their austerity
program will expand the American economy and thereby increase tax revenue, which is unlikely; and on the equally suspect
assumption that, if they get the economy up and the deficit

down, interest rates, and therefore the annual cost of servicing the debt, will go down—though this pattern has not been automatic in the past.

It is foolish for either party to claim that its particular fiscal package will definitely result in an absolute budget balance in five years, or seven or ten, when neither party can predict with any precision, much less control, the rate of interest or inflation or population growth or economic growth or other factors over that period of time. For the Republicans to include in their package measures that will impede growth and diminish demand, thereby turning some marginal taxpayers into "tax-eaters" and increasing the deficit still further, is particularly foolish. Those who have watched state governments resort to all kinds of legerdemain to declare their budgets "balanced" know how phony these statistical projections can be.

After all, the federal budget is merely a tool, a process, a set of accounts, one of many instruments that can help stimulate or slow down the national economy. For purposes of orderly and disciplined government, the budget should be in or close to balance in prosperous years, and even in lean years should be more under control than it has been during the last fifteen years. A government, like a family, must over the long run live within its limits. But balancing the budget in any particular year or set of years is not an end in itself, nor is it a test of the nation's economic strength, nor is it always a good idea, as Herbert Hoover discovered when his policies worsened the Great Depression. Most American families borrow—go into debt—to buy a house, a car, or some other major asset or meet the cost of a college tuition. So do most American companies when they undertake a major acquisition or new plant construction. Comparing debt to income and assets, our government is in better shape than the typical American family with a mortgage or the typical American company with a bond issue.

Our national debt, in short, justifies action and concern, but not cruelty or short-sightedness. To say that our wealthy nation cannot afford, for example, a long-term education plan—which would strengthen both national and family economic security—on the grounds that it will put this year's budget out of balance and require us to borrow, or might defer past 2002, the year when we will supposedly reduce the annual deficit to zero, simply makes no sense. Most of that debt is money we owe to ourselves. Much of it is money owed by one arm of the federal government to another. Most people do not believe that anything other than nasty ideology motivated the Republican budget's reduction or even elimination of tiny programs of little cost to the government but of vital importance to those dependent on them, such as recordings for the blind and dyslexic, or medical reimbursements for home oxygen, or scholarships for needy youngsters.

But voices of common sense and reason on this subject seem too often to be drowned out by a range of familiar, if unproven, assertions typically made by today's Republican leadership:

1. **"We must bring the deficit under control for the sake of the next generation."**

   Yes, but carefully. Demolishing education, health care, scientific research, student loans, and other services will not only hamper our economy and put more strains on the budget but, even worse, present to that next generation a far less livable society.

2. **"We must cut taxes now on the wealthy to increase the amount of funds that can be saved for investment."**

   Really? No predictably consistent pattern seems to tie our deplorably low savings rate to the rise and fall of our deficits, taxes, or even interest rates. The 1995 Republican tax bill would have increased consumption at the expense of savings while making no change in those long-standing tax code provisions that favor corporate and personal debt. Our economy today is indeed in need of private investment, but also public investment—in education, infrastructure, research, training, and other items cut by the Republicans.

3. **"We must balance the budget to relieve public anxiety."**

   The unspoken truth is that members of the public, with President Reagan's encouragement, created these budget deficits and continue to do so every year, demanding the same expenditures about which they are reportedly anxious and, more important, for which they do not want to pay. Getting the more responsible members of both parties, the media, and other opinion leaders to educate our way out of this inconsistent mind-set will not be easy, but is certainly preferable to trying to balance the budget on the backs of needy children and the elderly ill.

Permit me to make my position clear. Democrats are not spendthrifts, as the relatively restrained fiscal records of Kennedy,

Clinton, and other recent Democratic Presidents demonstrate. Today's Republicans assert that they are able and willing to cut both government programs and taxes more deeply, more quickly, and more ruthlessly than the Democrats. I do not challenge that. What I challenge is their sincerity when they justify those budget cuts by citing deficits that their own party amassed, and when they primarily focus those cuts on programs that help the poor and middle-class while leaving largely untouched programs that benefit their own constituents and campaign contributors. I further challenge their assertion that their primary goal in making these cuts is fiscal prudence, not conservative politics. Fiscal prudence does not require punishing the most vulnerable members of society.

I believe that today's Republican leaders and candidates might be coming much closer to the truth if they just came right out frankly and said:

> We don't really know whether our combination of budget cuts (hurting mostly the poor and middle class) and tax cuts (helping mostly corporations and those in the upper brackets) will get the deficit down to zero by 2002 or not. But we do know that we will be rolling back medical assistance, student loans, food stamps, and other programs that we have always been against, and that primarily serve people and employ people who do not vote for us anyway. In short, we are defunding the enemy with program cuts, and enriching our supporters with tax cuts. Not a bad political strategy. Saying we must do this in order to zero out the deficit in a particular year is as good a justification as any, because everyone is against the deficit.

Not a bad political strategy indeed. Its most vulnerable point is the inclusion in their fiscally austere "blame the deficit" package of a handsome tax cut for those who need it least. A quarter of a billion dollars taken out of Medicare can "pay for" an equally large cut in either income taxes or the deficit, but not both. A government forced to borrow over $200 billion a year to pay its bills should not now be yielding additional big chunks of its revenue through tax cuts for anyone, particularly the well-to-do.

Given the unlikelihood of the Republican plan's actually achieving its zero deficit goal, would not a true sense of fiscal discipline require postponement of a tax cut until that goal is neared? Or is a zero deficit not the Republicans' real goal? Would not a prudent approach to the nation's economic health argue in favor of saving such a cut until it is urgently needed to stimulate the economy? Inasmuch as the proposed Republican tax cut of 1995, though large enough to aggravate the deficit and the unhealthy disparities between the wealthy and everyone else, was too small to stimulate the economy anyway, what was its purpose, other than a reward to the Republicans' supporters? "Start salivating," *The Wall Street Journal* told its readers, "for the biggest tax-saving bonanza in years for upper income Americans"—more exemptions for those who could put large sums away, more cuts in the already favorable rate on capital gains (even on old investments), more tax shelters for corporations, more and still more for those who already had the most.

Next on the Republican agenda may be the so-called "flat tax," championed by multibillionaire Steve Forbes, which would effectively abolish the traditional rule of tax fairness that those who earn more and have more should pay more, called tax progressivity. By totally exempting all income received from dividends, interest, rent, and capital gains, and then taxing both high and low wages and salaries at the identical rate, the Republican flat tax proposal would sharply reduce taxes for big business and the rich while simultaneously raising the amount levied on those in every bracket except the over $200,000 group (and, incidentally, causing a gigantic, deficit-boosting, revenue shortfall)—all in the name of simplicity (we're all for that). Said a friend of moderate means, "I have often fantasized about what it would be like to be in the same income tax bracket as multibillionaire Bill Gates—but I never imagined it would happen without either of our incomes changing!" If the flat tax fails, the Republicans have proposals for a national sales tax or value-added tax, also tilted against progressivity, waiting in the wings.

We all wish we paid fewer taxes. But if we look around, we discover that we have been paying the lowest taxes in the developed world. The Republicans were not cutting taxes last year in order to make us more competitive with the Japanese and Germans, because citizens of those countries have long paid higher taxes than we do—particularly on the upper income brackets. The proportion of our gross domestic product (GDP) that goes to taxes—all taxes, federal and state, income and sales, and all the rest—was already below that of the other developed nations and has changed relatively little over the years.

The Republican tax bill of 1995, while closing almost no corporate and high-bracket loopholes and opening those loopholes still wider for capital gains and estate taxes, did raise taxes on one group of citizens—the working poor. The formerly bipartisan earned-income tax credit (EITC), which applied to working families with taxable incomes too low to benefit in full (or at all) from the per-child tax allowance, had successfully provided to those at the bottom of the ladder a modest incentive to get off and stay off welfare: they received a small tax credit or cash payment averaging little more than $1,000 to help them live above the poverty line. It is remarkable that these working men and women constituted the only bracket of taxpayers singled out by the Republicans for what was in effect a tax increase.

Once again, I can hear the reply: "He's waging class warfare . . . wants to redistribute the wealth!" Baloney. It ill becomes a political party whose tax bill favors the rich and penalizes the poor and whose budget slashes Medicare, Medicaid, food stamps, student loans, aid to dependent children, and child nutrition while continuing "corporate welfare" subsidies to accuse its opponents of class warfare. Furthermore, it requires no mathematical genius to calculate that the Republicans' rearrangement of the federal fiscal structure represents a striking redistribution of wealth—from both the poor and the middle class to the rich.

When the rich are allowed to pay less than their fair share of the tax burden and the poor are too poor to pay any share of that burden, it is clear who gets stuck with a disproportionate share of the burden.

Both parties have raised and lowered taxes over the last thirty-three years, but it is the Republicans who have done far more to increase the deficit. Republican campaign orators who still attempt to pin on Democrats the "tax and spend" label should be reminded that their party alone has earned the right to be called the party of "borrow and spend."

Nevertheless, Democrats must beware of playing the Republican popularity game of tax cuts, spending cuts, and deficit cuts on the Republican playing field, because they can always be trumped by Republicans slashing to the point of irresponsibility both services and taxes. An alternative Democratic fiscal policy should emphasize fairness, shared sacrifice, progressivity, and economic growth and should encourage greater savings and investment instead of consumption. A long-term Democratic program of fiscal restraint should reexamine not simply programs for the poor and elderly but all parts of the budget, including defense, corporate welfare, and even the large, New Deal and Great Society entitlement programs, the costs of which have been escalating beyond inflation. Better to entrust the modification and reform of those programs to the party that fathered them than to the party that always fought them.

Embarking upon that necessary reform will be a painful process, requiring political courage as well as responsibility. It would be much more comfortable politically to leave untouched the popular entitlement programs. It would certainly be much more "rewarding" politically to adopt what I firmly believe has been the Republican approach: tilting the fiscal package toward benefiting their own political support base. It is not surprising that Republican campaign coffers are now enjoying a record flood of sizable contributions from corporate political action committees (PACs) and the business and professional community. After all, as George Bernard Shaw once observed, any political body that "robs Peter to pay Paul can always depend on the support of Paul."

In the final analysis, the key question for Democrats in any debate over a particular budget item is not simply how much it can be cut, or even how much it costs, but how much good it does. Democratic programs that have helped educate and train Americans for better jobs, helped restore their health for longer lives, helped meet their needs for a fuller retirement, helped clean their air and water for a better environment—these are not simply dollars spent. They are investments in human capital that have paid huge dividends, strengthening our families and our economy, enriching our society, and enabling people to assume more responsibility for their own problems and to live out their lives in decency and dignity—all at a comparatively low cost. Our nation should stop borrowing so much at the expense of our children; but we should also start investing more in their future. Our party should stop being defensive about these essential expenditures it fostered, and start being proud of what those expenditures have achieved. I know that they make me proud—proud that I am a Democrat.

# ☆ CHAPTER 6 ☆
## LISTENING TO OUR CONSCIENCE
☆ ☆ ☆

*I am a champion of individual freedom and responsibility.* I do not want the government to tell me what to do and I do not expect the government to help me support my family. Descended from pioneers, I subscribe to the traditional American faith in the worth and dignity of individuals and their ability to make their own decisions and their own mistakes, to take their own risks and reap their own rewards, and to fully meet their own responsibilities at work and at home. All this, I am told, resonates with Republican dogma.

But there is more to a meaningful human existence than rugged individualism, every man for himself. Traditionally, in this country, "No man is an island," as the poet John Donne put it. We are each "a part of the main." We each have obligations not only to our families but also to our neighbors, our fellow citizens, our communities, our country. The very concept of community is based on reciprocal responsibilities, on giving something back to the society that has nurtured us. "For of everyone to whom much is given, much will be required" runs the passage from Luke that Rose Fitzgerald Kennedy pressed upon her children.

The performance of public service, in or out of government, inside or outside Washington, is one manifestation of that obligation. So is volunteering one's services to help an educational, religious, community, or other nonprofit institution, working for a candidate, donating to charity, performing good deeds, and fostering a thousand other "points of light," in George Bush's memorably apt phrase. So is support for government actions that use our collective resources to help take care of those who cannot take care of themselves, where private action is inappropriate or insufficient.

Contrary to House Republican Majority Leader Dick Armey's belief that "social responsibility is a euphemism for personal irresponsibility," Democrats believe that a pooling of our individual obligations and concerns through government action is often needed to supplement individual charity. Without a wide sense of social responsibility in this country, we would have only cold and indifferent governments—and few or no nonprofit institutions, no voluntary organizations teaching literacy or distributing food, no contributions of hard-earned dollars or leisure time to charitable groups. Politics confined to self-interest leads quickly to the politics of, by, and for the most powerful special interests. No social responsibility? What a harsh and cynical view of mankind.

Moral responsibility, a phrase often on Republican lips, does not mean merely supporting instead of abandoning one's own infant child or aged parent. It also includes a willingness to see one's tax dollars used to help strangers in a far-off state—whether they are victims of flood, fire, or failed economic or educational policies; of racial or gender discrimination or of crime; of careless parents or indifferent teachers or a host of other causes. Social responsibility, like individual responsibility, puts conscience and compassion ahead of self-interest and self-centeredness. Despite the scorn of some who consider that outlook soft-headed, old-fashioned, or otherworldly, conscience and compassion remain deeply ingrained in the philosophy of the Democratic Party.

In contrast, modern Republican politics, a long, long way from the party of Abraham Lincoln, has concerned itself too little with questions of conscience or compassion. The emphasis instead is all on hard numbers—number of voters who vote, number of dollars donated, number of congressmen elected. Simple arithmetic, we are frequently told, assures the success of Republican candidates for President and Congress for many years to come. Brutally simple arithmetic: there are far more whites than blacks in this country, far more employed than unemployed, far more conservative Protestants than Catholics, Jews, Muslems, and nonbelievers, far more taxpayers than "tax-eaters," far more physically firm than disabled, far more straights than gays, more gun owners than gun abolishers, and more voters residing outside the big cities than in them.

Still more simple Republican arithmetic: most poor people do not vote. Children cannot vote. Many African Americans do not vote. Neither do young people. Newly arrived immigrants cannot vote at all. And neither can the citizens of other countries looking to the United States for leadership.

With these numbers in mind, it is not difficult for Republican strategists, spin masters, and speechwriters to fashion a winning campaign for candidates whose principal (if not principled) appeal is to the politics of self-interest; who seek votes not on the basis of where we are headed or what must be done but of who gets what and how much; who appeal not so much to individual voters as to blocs, categories, and, above all, interest groups— economic, ethnic, religious, regional, and other interests, including in particular single-issue groups like the National Rifle Association and the antiabortion organizations. Groups the Republicans regard as "do-gooders," people who want to help the poor or the weak or the environment, are of much less importance to their leadership, despite their fondness for the phrase "moral responsibility." Indeed, Republican legislators seek to put limits on advocacy by most nonprofits and to cut off funding for many of them.

Such an approach assumes that people vote solely their own pocketbooks or other self-interest. It assumes that the employed are largely indifferent to the fate of the unemployed, that the white majority is largely indifferent to the concerns of the black minority, that voters dwelling outside declining urban areas are unaffected by what happens within those areas, that hardhearted men are more influential politically than concerned women, that taxpayers will always favor a tax cut at the expense of "tax-eaters," and that denouncing immigrants, foreign aid, and the United Nations is always safe. At the same time, says this strategy, keep identifying the Democratic Party with life's losers, those who lack money or jobs or good health, a good business or good luck.

The cynicism of that approach is not confined, as some might charitably argue, to the rough and tumble of electoral politics. In the introductory chapter to his book *Profiles in Courage,* John F. Kennedy recalled a senator ("retired," he fibbed, lest the identity of his source be guessed) who had acknowledged to him one day, during a roll-call vote, that "he voted with the special interests on every issue, hoping that by election time all of them added together would constitute nearly a majority that would remember him favorably, while the other members of the public would never know about—much less remember—his vote against their welfare." Those "special interests," J.F.K.'s source might have added, not only care more deeply and remember more surely but also contribute more readily; in addition, they are more likely to have lobbyists in Washington to influence and remind the senator how to vote correctly and to make certain that he does. This practice continues to be perfected in a Republican-controlled Congress, notwithstanding all the rhetoric of "revolutionary" change. The politics of self-interest leads inexorably to the politics of special interests.

Without denying that many individual Democrats are prone to pursue similarly cynical calculations, I firmly believe that our party on the whole has consistently taken a broader approach, appealing more often than the Republican Party to the voters' profounder instincts and wider concerns, to America's tradition of caring and common community interests, and not solely or even primarily to self-interest.

Of course, Democratic programs and proposals aimed at helping small business or small farmers, workers or consumers, the retired or the disabled, also offer direct benefits to those eligible—and, I believe, indirect benefits to all who have an economic or other stake in a stronger American economy, a more tranquil American society, and a more healthy, happy, and educated American people. But the Democratic Party also repeatedly asks its members and voters to support measures of national importance that may benefit them not at all, that may in fact be directly contrary to their best short-term business or personal economic interests—and to support such a measure not out of fear for the consequences of its defeat, not out of some grudging loyalty to the Democratic Party, but because the enactment of that measure, whether it is righting an old wrong, or helping those who hurt, or preserving our national honor, is plainly and simply the right and necessary thing to do. And most Democrats give this support.

We are, in short, a party reflecting character as well as calculation, values as well as interests, moral as well as material goals, and human as well as statistical projections, and we must continue to be so.

That is why congressional Democrats have so often, on these issues that test both goodness and toughness, voted to help people who will not turn out to vote for them, and enacted programs contributing to the subsistence of people too needy to contribute to campaigns. That is why the Democratic Party has traditionally championed consumers against those who would defraud or overcharge them, workers against those who would exploit them, tenants against those who would mistreat them, and all those whom ill health or ill winds have made more vulnerable to the vicissitudes of life: the very old and the very young, people of color and people in need, the disabled and the disadvantaged, those trying to lift themselves and better their lives. Such people may not be able to make campaign contributions or speeches. Their pictures may not appear in the newspapers. Their names or accents may not be familiar. But they are still our sisters and brothers.

When Republicans talk about "responsibility," they mean each person must shoulder his or her own burdens. When Democrats talk about "responsibility," we include the obligations of all citizens—each student and teacher, each worker and manager, each parent and policeman—acting alone and acting through civic organizations and government, to ask what they can do for their country, for their fellow humans, for the less fortunate, less powerful, and more vulnerable. Ever since Franklin Roosevelt—who, Joseph Alsop wrote, "included the excluded"—reached out to the powerless, the helpless, and the hopeless, ours has been an inclusive party, welcoming individuals of every kind and view. Colin Powell no doubt came to realize that the Republican Party has increasingly become an exclusive party, antiblack, antilabor, antiintellectual, antiartist, antifeminist, antigay, anticity, antigovernment, and antienvironmentalist. There are, of course, a few token members of each group in the Republican ranks, but essentially it remains the party of, by, and for white businessmen, with voting muscle supplied by the right-wing Christian Coalition and the NRA gun lobby.

Elsewhere in this book I emphasize the differences between the parties in terms of programs, projects, and price tags. But prices are not values, and the difference in values of which I write in this chapter is equally important, if not more so. Speaker Gingrich declared in his book that our nation's values, not our economics, face a crisis. In fact, both face a crisis, and those crises are intertwined: the inequities produced by stagnant wages, the insecurities spawned by global competition, the unfairness of tax loopholes, the irresponsibility of shredding the safety net.

Anyone doubting these basic differences in values and viewpoints between the two major parties need only look at the differences in who benefits from and who is hurt by the Republican fiscal and legislative approach compared to who benefits from and who is hurt by the comparable Democratic package. Not many wealthy suburbanites have been directly hurt by Republican budget cuts. Not many inner-city or rural poor have been helped by Republican tax cuts.

Or look at the difference in each party's list of supporters. The Republican list includes the most powerful lobbies in Washington: the health insurance lobby, the chemical industry lobby, the tobacco growers' and manufacturers' lobby, the gun, banking, utilities, mining, grazing, petroleum, timber, and hundreds of other lobbies. In their battle to lower the deficit, the Republicans "are very good at taking on the poor and the lame, but not . . . the muscle guys," said Congressman Dave Obey of Wisconsin. The Democrats also have support from lobbyists: the environmental lobby, the children's defense lobby, the consumer, labor, civil rights, and other organizations, well intended if not always well financed, representing not large industries but ordinary people.

And who, also by way of comparison, are the people to whom the Democrats over the years have extended a helping hand? Ever since the "Hundred Days" of F.D.R., they have traditionally been collectively summarized in such phrases as the "forgotten man" (forgotten by the privileged and powerful), the "common man" (neither uncommonly rich nor uncommonly powerful), the "little people" (too little to lobby for tax loopholes), the "average worker," the "typical family," the "ordinary everyday people." To my knowledge, none of those terms has ever been plausibly used to describe either the supporters or the beneficiaries of modern Republican Party policies.

To be compassionate and humanitarian, Democrats are now advised by both columnists and campaign consultants, is "out," "passé," "history." Ronald Reagan, said former New York governor Mario Cuomo, "made the denial of compassion respectable." The undeserving poor don't deserve it, say the Republicans; those without earnings haven't earned it; cutting off their food stamps and cash assistance is for their own good.

These same kibitzers further advise the Democrats never to blame anyone's plight on failed national trade or health or other policies, or on adverse economic trends or innate institutional prejudice; that's excusing victims for not meeting their responsibilities. Never call attention to economic inequities or social injustices; that's running down America and engaging in "class warfare." And never attack corporate and other special-interest PACs for selfish demands, whatever their sins against the public interest; for they are the source from which most campaign blessings flow.

If the Democrats fall for this advice and hold their fire, if they forget the "forgotten men and women" in their own pursuit of wealthy donors, if they abandon the politics of broad-based values for the politics of narrow interest groups, if they drop the drive to improve health care, housing, education, job training, and the environment, then they will lose their very purpose in politics, even if they win more elections.

That would not be the Democratic Party I know and serve. "How are things?" an acquaintance was once reported to have asked writer James Thurber, to which he replied, "Things? I don't care about things. I care about people." The Democratic Party cares about people, "little" people as well as big, underdogs as well as top dogs, and even losers as well as winners. That is a major reason why I am a Democrat.

# ☆ CHAPTER 7 ☆
## UNITING OUR PEOPLE
☆ ☆ ☆

*I am an angry white male.* Inasmuch as my grandparents came to this country long after slavery ended, and my parents and spouse and siblings and I have always fought racism, I see no reason why my racial identity alone should burden me with some kind of collective guilt for the centuries of mistreatment that black Americans have suffered at the hands of whites. When blacks are found guilty of criminal conduct, whether corruption in high office or petty thuggery on the street, I see no reason why their experiences with racial discrimination or poverty should excuse them any more than whites for such offenses. I see no reason why blacks engaging in anti-Semitic remarks, or boycotting a neighborhood grocery because the owner is Korean, are any less guilty of racism than whites protesting a black home owner in their neighborhood solely because of his or her color.

If the black lawyers in my law firm had been admitted to law school, to the New York Bar, or to our office solely to meet some rigid numerical and arbitrary racial quota, not because they were immensely talented, I would have been profoundly disturbed. If an able white professor were called "racist" solely for denouncing his being replaced by an unqualified black hired under just such a quota, in an act of blatant reverse discrimination, I would deem that label wholly unjustified. If the Republican Party were right in arguing that the Democratic Party is extending affirmative action programs for political reasons only, and that such programs require employers to hire unqualified blacks instead of more qualified whites, I would be angry at my party. I would fully understand those white males, particularly in the South, who have deserted the Democrats in droves.

But, in fact, not one of these hypotheses is true. I am angry, instead, because, more than thirty years after John F. Kennedy declared that "race has no place in American life or law," racism is on the rise once again in this country. I am angry because our economy is weakened for everyone, and our country's moral leadership is weakened everywhere, by our failure to utilize to the fullest the abilities and energies of every American. I am angry that the Republican Party, for partisan campaign purposes, has succeeded in slyly introducing a racial subtext into so many legislative issues—the safety net, crime, education, housing, and many others—and has succeeded as well in distorting the meaning and purpose of affirmative action programs. I am angry that the Republicans have been largely successful in focusing public discomfort over affirmative action solely on blacks and minorities, trying to erase from the voter's mind the millions of white women whose equal opportunity has been enhanced by these same outreach policies.

I have never doubted that some affirmative action programs, like almost any human endeavor, have been subject to abuses that need correction; I know that race-based contract set-asides and tax breaks are often improperly exploited by white business-men who use blacks as fronts and pass-throughs. I believe that those affirmative action programs (usually court-ordered or corporate-sponsored) that do require group quotas and prefer-ences for unqualified minorities or women, resulting in reverse discrimination, should be reconsidered and restructured. But I do not believe that the playing field has been so leveled now for all Americans seeking education or employment opportunities, re-gardless of race or gender, that all such extra efforts can be ended, as the Republicans maintain.

White males, less than half of the labor force, still hold more than 95 percent of top corporate and government jobs, and their companies still receive roughly that proportion of government contracts. They still control the vast proportion of the nation's wealth, political and governmental bodies, media, financial mar-kets, and police forces. They suffer half the rate of unemployment as black men, and consistently receive substantially higher wages and salaries than blacks, and this is so even at lower skill and occupational levels, where blacks have virtually closed the gap in high school dropout and graduation rates. Even in today's col-lege-oriented economy, the average black college graduate is more likely to be unemployed than the average white high school graduate. The average black American is far more likely than the average white American to die by murder or in infancy, to live in poverty, to attend a poor school, to work in a dead-end job, to earn half as much money, and to end up either legally jailed or illegally assaulted by white policemen.

How, then, can the Republicans pretend or profess to believe that racial discrimination has ended, that equal opportunity has arrived, and that affirmative action is no longer needed? According to official complaints filed with federal and state equal employment opportunity commissions, the number of complaints of reverse discrimination against white males is less than one thirtieth of the total. Despite all the progress of the last thirty-five or more years, I have never heard of a white who, after complaining about preferences for blacks or handouts for blacks or "free rides" for blacks, was willing, in order to obtain those supposed benefits, to change the color of his own skin. Why not? Because he would thereby sharply diminish his prospects of ever escaping poverty, becoming a professional, or owning his own home. To cite just one statistic: black home mortgage applicants are twice as likely to be denied a mortgage as white applicants with the same assets and credit standing.

For too many years the national Democratic Party, unwilling to drive out the white Southern segregationists who delivered electoral college and congressional majorities, temporized on the issues of civil rights and tolerated an alliance with Jim Crow. But ever since 1948, when President Harry Truman and Minneapolis Mayor Hubert Humphrey declared that human rights should be placed ahead of states' rights; ever since 1963, when John F. Kennedy fought for "every American's right to vote, to go to school, to get a job and to be served in a public place without arbitrary discrimination . . . not merely for reasons of economic efficiency, world diplomacy, and domestic tranquillity— but, above all, because it is right"; and ever since 1964 and 1965, when Lyndon Johnson signed, expanded, and strengthened Kennedy's civil rights legislation and regulations, that Democratic alliance with Jim Crow has ended. Two Southern Democratic Presidents, Jimmy Carter and Bill Clinton, who knew first hand the political and social penalties in their region for holding liberal views on race, continued this effort to level the playing field for all Americans.

Exactly as Lyndon Johnson predicted, the Democratic Party has paid a high political price for doing what was right. Its presidential candidates, even those from the South, have been unable to carry the South. White Democratic voters and officeholders have increasingly turned Republican, particularly in the South. New white voters in the South have increasingly registered as Republicans, now that they have two viable parties to choose from and retirements have diminished the congressional seniority advantages of voting Democratic.

The Democratic Party's leaders, to their everlasting credit, under attack from within the party's ranks as well as without, stood their ground. As a result, in the South today for the first time since Reconstruction, the majority of governors, senators, and U.S. representatives are Republican. The Democratic Party in the South, once overwhelmingly white and successful, at least in part because of the national party's hesitance on "the race issue," is becoming overwhelmingly black and unsuccessful, at least in part because of the current national party's courage on this same issue. Nor is the drain of white voters away from the Democratic Party because of this issue limited to the South. Nearly two thirds of my fellow white males nationwide, at least some of whom were influenced by the Republican bombardment on affirmative action, voted Republican in the 1994 congressional elections.

The Republican Party, once the party of Abraham Lincoln, once the party whose congressional leaders largely responded to Kennedy's and Johnson's calls by joining in the passage of the nation's most far-reaching civil rights legislation ever, has become in more recent years the party that has cleverly and successfully exploited these growing racial and geographic divisions among the Democrats. I exonerate and salute moderate Republicans who have no bias in their bones and no flaws in their civil rights records, as well as realistic and concerned conservatives like Jack Kemp. I sympathize with that lonely handful of black Republicans. (Last year, the Virginia Republican Party sponsored a rally in Richmond's largest hall to attract black voters to the party. Six thousand prominent blacks were invited. Nine came.) But I cannot forgive the Republican majority for further dividing America along racial lines, not for racist reasons—I believe relatively few of them are actually racists—but solely for political purposes. I cannot forgive them for joining with the likes of Louis Farrakhan in not only sowing but cultivating the seeds of separatism and mutual distrust in this country.

Richard Nixon expanded affirmative action well beyond the Kennedy-Johnson rules by imposing hiring quotas in the construction industry; he did this at least in part, we now learn from his staff's diaries, to pit labor and blacks against each other for the benefit of the Republican cause. But he artfully employed the race issue for campaign purposes in what he called his "Southern strategy." Ronald Reagan, whose Department of Justice and judicial appointees made it respectable once again in Republican and Southern circles to favor segregated schools and cut back civil rights, opened his own Southern presidential campaign by signaling his willingness to return to "states' rights" on this issue. In both the North and South, George Bush's campaign for the White House used the infamous, racist, and widely televised commercial associating a black criminal, Willie Horton, with Bush's Democratic opponent. And today's congressional Republicans, led by Newt Gingrich and Bob Dole, neither man a knowing racist, have tragically if not intentionally increased the polarization of the country along racial lines by denouncing, distorting, inaccurately redefining, and calling for the end of affirmative action.

Opposing affirmative action, like opposing busing twenty years ago, has become the code word for politicians wishing to signal to their constituents that they oppose civil rights for blacks and minorities in general. Affirmative action has been called the "wedge issue" of the 1996 campaign, and rightfully so, since the Republicans hope to use it not only to divide Republicans from Democrats, particularly along racial lines, but to divide Democrats from Democrats as well.

The Republicans have done this in part by blaming on blacks and affirmative action the white worker's job insecurity and wage stagnation, which have actually been caused, as noted earlier, by unrelated long-term economic trends. They have also done it by distorting our party's own traditional civil rights terminology. In my dictionary, bringing to the table someone never before allowed to eat there is not "preferential treatment." "Color-blind" never meant blind to the hate and handicap automatically directed toward some people because of their color. "Goals and timetables" such as the legislative goals and timetables set forth in the Contract With America are not "quotas." Determining "individual rights" never required ignoring the centuries of discrimination imposed upon all individual members of the group into which that individual was born. A "preference" that helps the disadvantaged cannot logically or legally be equated with a "preference" that further hurts them. And for those who have at best averted their gaze from racism and sexism throughout their political careers to now accuse Democrats of having introduced "group consciousness" into our politics smacks of hypocrisy.

So I, too, am a white male who is angry. I am particularly

angry because I had a hand in the first affirmative action initiative, an executive order by President Kennedy in 1961 requiring federal contractors to make special good-faith outreach efforts, measured by reasonable and realistic guidelines, with goals and timetables but no quotas, in order to ensure that those contractors' employees were hired and promoted without regard to race. In the absence of that extra effort, we were convinced, workers from one segment of our citizenry too often would have been excluded from jobs financed with public funds provided by all segments of our citizenry—a wholly indefensible state of affairs under the most minimal standards of fairness.

That was a very modest and moderate start in tackling a very large and long-standing evil. But it represented an important first step that could be initiated without the participation of a Congress filled with powerful Southern Democrats. President Johnson expanded Kennedy's executive order to cover women as well and to include educational institutions, nonfederal employment, and housing. President Nixon enlarged it further, authorizing quotas for the first time and giving affirmative action a bipartisan stamp. A variety of court orders, often to counter stubborn defiance, went still further, as did the separate programs of various independent agencies, state and local governments, and efforts initiated by the business and academic communities. While this process of expansion no doubt occasioned some excesses and departures from the original effort of 1961, that effort's basic intention still lies at the heart of affirmative action.

What, then, does affirmative action truly mean?

- Not one group's entitlement to particular jobs, but each individual's equal opportunity to have his and her individual merits fairly known and considered.

- Not a guarantee of equal results in life—admission to school or to a first job is hardly a final result—but of a more equal opportunity for a productive life.
- Not an ethnic or gender quota that picks unqualified persons over qualified persons, but a process that assures qualified females and persons of color an opportunity to make known and make use of their qualifications.
- Not new discrimination against white males, but an end to the centuries of discrimination against females and nonwhites in favor of white males.
- Not an insistence on numerical results, even in a grossly lopsided situation, but insistence on a remedial approach.
- Not lower or suspended standards for some applicants, but, for the first time, a single standard for all applicants, sometimes supplemented by special programs to bring all educationally deprived aspirants up to that single standard.
- Not charity for the mediocre but a reward for newly visible excellence.
- Not a burden on society, but a means of reducing the cost to society of its needlessly unproductive members.
- Not a means of systematically guaranteeing equal or even equitable representation of nonwhites and females in a workforce or student body, but of sidestepping systems that guaranteed no equal or equitable representation.
- Not the introduction of racial preferences into the selection system, but the elimination of these preferences.
- Not reparations or compensation for the past, but a sustained commitment to override its effects and enrich the future.

- In summary, a sustained commitment to promote fairness and justice where unfairness and injustice had previously reigned.

These are, of course, mere words, objectives, and intentions, although they are also legal criteria consistent with the latest Supreme Court decision on this issue. But that decision—like *every* decision that the Court has handed down on affirmative action—was neither unanimous nor crystal clear as to its consequences. Every affirmative action plan or decision should meet these tests; but every lawyer knows that in practice such tests are more easily asserted than assured.

The record so indicates. On the one hand, individual agencies, courts, and employers have fashioned specific plans from time to time that did not meet these ideal standards, to the detriment of white male applicants; those plans should now be rewritten. On the other hand, the persistent gaps in black and white educational and employment opportunities today make clear that thirty-five years of affirmative action plans have still not come close to eliminating school and job discrimination based on race. They have been of very little help to inner-city youngsters who have already attended too many badly run, badly financed ghetto schools, who have foreseen in their home communities the kind of life and death that awaited them, and who have been swept too far away from the mainstream ever to become part of it.

Some affirmative action programs, as noted earlier, need to be better administered or better worded. The new effort to expand affirmative action programs on a race-neutral basis to reach out to all those who have been unfairly deprived, regardless of color and gender, should be fully tested. Race-neutral programs that address the problems of all the truly disadvantaged will especially benefit minorities deprived by decades of racial subjugation. But none of this justifies the Republican call for the immediate and total abolition of all affirmative action programs. Affirmative action remains a messy, imperfect solution in a messy, imperfect world that offers no better solution.

Far from totally failing, as alleged by its critics, affirmative action programs—often their mere existence—have helped to open previously closed doors to countless numbers of individuals whose talents had earlier been invisible, buried under impenetrable layers of prejudice and discrimination: black army officers now commanding mostly white troops, black professionals now advising white as well as black clients, female business executives leading male and female managers, public officials of every gender and hue, integrated police departments more respected in all neighborhoods, technicians, electricians, computer programmers, astronauts, doctors, lawyers—all of us know and have benefited at least indirectly from endless examples of affirmative action's success. None of these successful individuals lacked the innate talents to excel—they lacked access to compete. The mainstream of the American economy has been enlarged and enriched by these new and diverse streams, formerly blocked but now flowing into it. Previously less productive workers are now contributing more to our economy.

For every white male (and there are many) who grumbles that affirmative action can only do him harm, there are dozens of other white males working for companies that, as a result of affirmative action, are all the stronger and more productive, and are hiring more workers, because they are now able to draw upon a larger pool of skills or to sell to a larger market of customers or to bring in new ideas or perspectives from a broader universe. For every such complaint, there are also dozens of other white males who work for educational institutions or government agencies that, as a result of affirmative action, have gained more effectiveness, pride, and popular appeal through more representative diversity in the ranks of their employees.

For every individual black worker (and there are many) who feels demeaned, tainted, or suspect, because his white coworkers may incorrectly assume that he did not obtain his job on merit, there are dozens of other blacks now enabled to fully advance in the mainstream of the economy, to reach for a business, professional, or other upwardly mobile career that previously was beyond their grasp because of unfair and artificial barriers, and who now are able to serve as role models and counselors for younger aspiring blacks. In our largely segregated society, affirmative action has also resulted in more people of different races working and lunching and talking and studying together. Without this interaction, the fierce racial tensions, divisions, and resentments in this country—exposed once again last year by the O. J. Simpson trial—might well have exploded.

Affirmative action need not be a zero-sum game. For example, the federal Small Business Administration has been able to increase its loans to businesswomen and minority business owners without reducing the number of loans made to white male business owners and without lowering its standards. Affirmative action has expanded the size of the middle class, not knocked white males out of it. Countless black and Latino students admitted to colleges despite the measurable effects on their entry test scores of prolonged social, economic, and educational discrimination have, once given a chance, gone on to academic and professional leadership.

The Republicans, who think constantly in terms of limits and ceilings, view blacks as "them," not "us," and apparently believe that every new black job above the menial labor level is a job taken away from whites, and that every black college student is occupying the desk of a displaced white. Not true. Democrats, in contrast, believe our economy, our payrolls, and our higher education systems can and should and will be expanded, and that affirmative action increases the productivity and demand that will help to bring about that expansion, with better jobs, better pay, and better education for all who are willing to work hard, whatever their color or gender.

In a land of true equal opportunity—and much more than affirmative action will be required to get us there—these programs might well become unnecessary. In a land of pure meritocracy, some extended forms of affirmative action might well be deemed a violation of that principle. But let's be frank. I know of no school, employer, union, or even government agency that does not judge applicants at least in part on the basis of one or more considerations other than merit (which usually means standardized test scores). These include parental or official influence, athletic prowess, physical appearance, inside contacts, connections, politics, geography, and precedents. In fact, companies and schools committed and sensitive to the principles of affirmative action are likely to be diverted less often from merit by any irrelevant and artificial considerations, including but not limited to race and gender; they are thereby better, stronger institutions than those that have no such programs.

Moreover, while standardized test scores may roughly measure academic preparation, the true list of "merit qualifications" for most schools, jobs, and promotions also includes creativity, honesty, interpersonal skills, motivation, courage, uniqueness, perseverance, persuasiveness, and performance. To rely solely on test scores would be folly.

In short, I do not agree with those, black or white, who say that affirmative action has been a total failure, or who say, going still further, that little or nothing has been accomplished under more than thirty years of significant civil rights laws. The hopes and dreams of which Martin Luther King, Jr., eloquently spoke in the summer of 1963 are far from being completely realized. Nevertheless, far more blacks have better jobs and incomes than they did thirty years ago. Far more go to better schools and hospitals, live in better homes and neighborhoods, participate in more elections, hold more public offices, and eat in better restaurants—and in doing all of these things encounter less white resistance and violence.

Too much segregation, discrimination, racism, fear, tension, and resentment remain for anyone, white or black, to take much satisfaction from this record. This country has a long way to go before it can fulfill the pledge we all took every day in public school to the flag of a United States of America "with liberty and justice for *all*," not merely for the white, rich, and native-born. But we can take pride in the fact that our country has made a more sweeping, courageous, and effective attack on racial and ethnic discrimination than any other country on earth.

In this chapter I have focused on discrimination against blacks because they have been victimized the worst and longest and are at the center of the national political debate on this issue. But the arbitrary denial of equal educational and economic opportunities to Hispanics or Latinos, to Native Americans, Asian Americans, and others is no less repugnant in a free society. In addition, the continuing need for antidiscrimination measures to protect American women of every ethnic background is undeniable, particularly in the job market. Affirmative action's greatest success has come in helping women—mostly those who could afford it—

to gain graduate degrees and placement as business managers, lawyers, doctors, and engineers. But despite these gains, and despite the splendid example set by Presidents Carter and Clinton in their own appointments, women still occupy only a tiny fraction of the top executive positions in our major companies.

In their new professional roles and even more so in the "pink-collar" jobs to which most of them are still relegated as secretaries, nurses, teachers, computer operators, and other posts that are as essential to our economy as comparable occupations dominated by men, women are consistently paid less than their male counterparts for the same amount of hard work, training, and skill. This is particularly true when white women are compared with white men. Most Republican opponents of continuing affirmative action remain quiet about its importance to white working women, but opinion surveys increasingly show that those women know who their real political adversary is

The Republican-led assault against affirmative action has been accompanied by a similarly nasty campaign against immigrants.

As the grandson of immigrants living in a nation composed almost entirely of immigrants and descendants of immigrants, I am appalled by the spectacle of the Republican Party, in its search for scapegoats for our present economic worries, singling out legal immigrants—legal immigrants, who are working (often at two menial jobs), paying taxes, waiting out the bureaucratically prolonged naturalization process, serving in our armed forces, and helping build consumer demand for our products, but not yet, of course, eligible to vote.

I am not talking about illegal immigrants, immigration fraud, anachronistic eligibility requirements, the already forbidden entry of "those likely to become a public charge," the issuance of temporary work permits or guest-worker cards to fill jobs that unemployed Americans are willing and able to fill, or the entry of elderly parents on the basis of assurances from their naturalized adult children, who subsequently abandon them. Almost all Americans oppose these practices, oppose illegal immigration, want our borders better protected, acknowledge that our country cannot accommodate everyone who wants to move here, and support improved enforcement and legislative reform along the lines recommended by the commission headed by the late and beloved former congresswoman Barbara Jordan.

But over the years, this country has never failed to be enriched by the contributions of highly motivated legal immigrants awaiting citizenship. Some have been the highly skilled and specially admitted: famous scientists, doctors, engineers, and artists. Others have contributed in myriad ways to building America's society, economy, and culture, including those who have worked in farmers' fields that might otherwise go unharvested and those who have worked for career women with children who would otherwise go unattended. Studies show that legal immigrants have on average actually paid more taxes and received fewer benefits than their native-born counterparts. We do not judge Americans on the basis of when they or their forebears arrived in this country. Yet the Republicans have urged that these citizens-in-waiting lose their constitutional right as "persons" in America; they would be denied access to public services, eligibility for college student grants and loans, protection by the public safety net (such as Medicaid and Food Stamps), and even access to our public schools, once and still the great loci of Americanization.

The Republicans are also urging that children of legal immigrants who arrive in public school unable to understand a standard English-language curriculum no longer be given the choice of being gradually weaned away from dependence on their native tongue through bilingual education. Universal use of the English language within our country is without a doubt a key to economic, educational, and civic success and harmony. But those goals are not automatically advanced by forcing all immigrant schoolchildren immediately into English-only, sink-or-swim classes that cannot make allowances for linguistic handicaps, cannot measure different levels of progress, and cannot counteract the frustrations, failures, dropouts, and resentments that all too surely follow.

Penalizing children who have not yet mastered English is consistent with the paranoid Republican fear that too many foreigners are "altering the nature" of this country, even though the percentage of foreign-born here today is far below early-twentieth-century levels, when European Jews and Irish Catholics were the perceived threat to American society. No doubt cultural diversity still seems threatening to some, and some "politically correct" higher education facilities do seem determined to carry the pursuit of diversity to absurd extremes, blotting out or demeaning large chunks of America's history and roots in the process. But it is equally extreme to pretend in a country boasting of its many tongues and accents, and its global variety of customs and culinary treats, that we are all descended from Revolutionary War heroes, or even that their heritage was not a mixed one.

Too many restrictions on the lawful entry to our shores of those fleeing persecution, repression, or starvation would truly fundamentally "alter the nature" and role of this historic haven of democratic freedom and opportunity. It is true that the presence of large numbers of poor legal immigrants in this country can have an adverse impact at the bottom of our economic pyramid, as well as a beneficial impact elsewhere. But to the extent that such immigration facilitates lower wages, unemployment, or discrimination against poor Americans at the labor-force entry level, that is simply an additional reason to strengthen our minimum-wage laws, our public works and other job-creation programs—and affirmative action.

Some Republican opponents of affirmative action are concealing a much larger agenda of reversing all the major civil rights gains of the last half century. Other Republicans are cynically courting these extremists, citing as justification the inevitable flaws and abuses in some affirmative action programs but offering no corrections or substitutes. Still other opponents actually do not care about affirmative action or the unmistakably hostile message that abandoning it would send, aiming their sights only on winning more elections and more recruits to the Republican ranks. They may well succeed. Affirmative action, particularly when ill defined, is an easy target for distortion and demagoguery.

But if this country is to be true to its ideals, it cannot retreat from any of its principles of civil rights and affirmative action. Nor can the Democratic Party, for the same reason. Through patient, thoughtful explication and definition, such as Senator Bill Bradley's and President Clinton's major addresses on the subject, Democrats can make race a less divisive issue. By undertaking new initiatives to end wage and salary stagnation and the escalating wealth gap, they can make it a less dominant issue. Despite these efforts, like it or not, race in this country—or, more accurately, the disparity in economic, political, and human rights and power among the races in this country—promises to be the most divisive, most difficult issue facing our political leaders for years to come; and most of them would simply prefer not to face it.

I do not blame them. I truly wish that race relations were not a major issue between the parties, even if it ultimately becomes an issue that helps instead of hurting the Democrats. I truly wish that nine out of ten black voters in this country were not being driven into the ranks of one party only, even if that party is the Democratic Party, because that encourages white Democratic leaders to take the black vote for granted and frees white Republican leaders to play all their "race cards." I truly wish that race did not need to be considered in fairly configuring Southern and other congressional districts to assure at least a modicum of blacks in Congress, even if most of those black congressmen are Democrats. I truly wish that the so-called Balkanization of American politics, the fragmentation generated by campaigns in both parties that make separate pitches for each racial, ethnic, and other demographic category of voters, would cease forever, even if the practitioners of that appeal include some skillful black and white Democrats.

Granting to every human being, regardless of color, a life of equal opportunity, dignity, and decency should be a moral issue in this country, not a political issue, not even an economic or social issue. Whatever the political consequences today, I am deeply proud of the Democratic Party for being willing to stand up on this moral issue.

But let no one underestimate the social and economic as well as political consequences of failing to meet this moral challenge. The increasingly small world in which we live and make our living is a world of diversity. If the United States of America, the most diverse of the economically advanced countries in the world, cannot convert its diversity from weakness to strength, if we cannot unshackle the racial and ethnic chains that bind the feet of our economy, if we cannot eliminate the racial and ethnic strains that sap our strength and threaten our stability, then every

American's future is bleak. It is said that affirmative action has been an unqualified success in the U.S. Army because every soldier recognizes that survival is more important than skin color and that survival is utterly dependent on teamwork and collaboration. I believe the same is true for our country.

We must come together. Given the all too frequent antiblack political and legislative tactics of the Republican Party over the last few decades, I doubt that a Republican President can bring us together. But given the Democratic Party's courage and conscience on issues of race, and its capacity to win the confidence of black and white, North and South, I believe a Democratic President can. That is another reason why I am a Democrat.

# ☆ CHAPTER 8 ☆
## COMBINING OUR EFFORTS
☆ ☆ ☆

*I have lived most of my life far from Washington, D.C.* Even during my years there, I never believed that all political power and tax money should flow to Washington, or that the only acceptable wisdom flows from there. I have always believed that the federal system by which the Framers divided sovereign authority between the states and central government was a work of genius as well as compromise, and I have long regarded Thomas Jefferson, an early foe of concentrated governmental power, as one of my political heroes. As the son and brother of onetime state officials, and the spouse and father of onetime local officials, I do not believe that large national bureaucracies in Washington necessarily know more than state and local leaders about state and local needs. During the twenty out of twenty-four years between 1968 and 1993 that Republicans controlled the executive branch of the federal government, I noticed that many of the most innovative advances on a small scale attacking poverty and urban decay came from Democratic governors and mayors, often in partnership with local business, and I oppose any national overcentralization of government that stifles local interest and participation.

I also believe that Washington should not be given unlimited authority to decide, force, or block state and local actions on matters appropriately left largely in local hands, such as criminal justice and law enforcement, school administration and finance, property taxes, fire prevention, trash collection, and community development, to cite only a few examples. I deplored the growing tendency of Congress, understandably concerned about waste and abuse, to keep such a tight rein on federal grants to state and local governments that it increasingly shaped them in the form of hundreds of highly specific, narrowly focused "categorical" grants, tied to thousands of federal conditions and millions of federal forms, many of which required a participating state to spend more money than the grants conveyed.

For these reasons, the Republican call for the "devolution" of some federal powers downward to the states appeared to have some merit. But once again, the Republican Congress went too far. In its zeal, it undertook literally to break up the federal government, to splinter its nationwide standards, policies, regulations, functions, and fiscal powers and to transfer authority for the safety net, the environment, health care, and a host of other national responsibilities to the fifty states. Far from acting to check waste, fraud, and abuse at the state level, where historically it has been more rampant than in Washington, the Congress envisioned each governor and legislature reigning supreme, each state largely setting its own standards, enforcing its own rules, without regard to its neighbors' or the nation's concerns, under a system not so different from the old Articles of Confederation that almost destroyed our infant nation before the Constitution was adopted in response.

I may be a resident of New York, but I am a citizen of the United States. *E pluribus unum:* From many, one. I have obligations to my fellow citizens, regardless of where they live, and my family's well-being is ultimately affected by what happens to those other citizens, regardless of where they live. I may resent the fact that year after year New Yorkers send more tax dollars to Washington and thus to the other forty-nine states than ever return in the form of federal expenditures—despite New York's greater need than most other states for help in combating poverty and other national problems. But I cannot be indifferent to the fate of other Americans who live in other states. Charles Wilson, the General Motors executive who became Eisenhower's secretary of defense, was rightly skewered for stating, "What's good for General Motors is good for the country." But he was absolutely right in the overlooked second half of that epigram: "And what's good for the country is good for General Motors." Because what's good for the country is good for every corporate and individual citizen in this country, including you and me. Conversely, whatever's bad for America, regardless of the state in which it occurs, is bad for every American. Inadequate schools in Mississippi are bad for New York. The spread of AIDS in New York is bad for Mississippi.

Without the assurance of reasonable uniformity in the basic rights, safeguards, and standards applicable in every state to the life, liberty, and the pursuit of happiness of every citizen, the threat of American Balkanization becomes more real than theoretical. When my wife has a speaking appearance in another part of the country, or my children or grandchildren move to new jobs or colleges in different states, I take comfort in knowing that uniform federal regulations, standards, and inspections assure the quality and safety of the airplane on which they fly, or the water they drink, the medical-care system they adopt, the workplace in which they labor, the automobile or medication they purchase, or the public schools their children attend. A state neglecting the health, education, and happiness of its citizens, or the safety of its streets, or the purity of the food it produces, or the adequacy of its transport and communications, can affect the quality of life of every citizen in every other state.

This is one country of closely united states, a principle that needs constant reiteration and renewal. In all of the American people's wondrous diversity, we are one people, with one national purpose and culture, working in one national economy, forming one national market. Thus, so long as federal funds are apportioned wisely and fairly, I do not object to my tax money helping to strengthen all regions and all people in this country.

Extraordinary developments in transportation, communication, and infrastructural technology have made this huge nation much smaller; the concept of community encompasses much more: effectively the whole nation. Few problems of significance are or long remain wholly state or local problems. They become or reflect national problems, not New York's or Nebraska's but America's problems, faced by citizens in many or all states. Natural disasters, crime, pollution, infection, and recession are but examples of problems that have no respect for state boundaries, and no state can solve them alone. National problems require national remedies, national strategies, national policies, standards and, resources. These United States were united in order to achieve great national missions, not to squabble over which jurisdiction gets what share of the national pie.

If the state of California but no other state had been invaded after Pearl Harbor, the American people would not have considered permitting California to face the invader alone. If the state of Florida had sought to operate its own separate Medicare system, or the states of North and South Dakota had wanted to install their own separate fair labor standards acts, or if thirty-five years ago each state had contemplated establishing its own space program, we would not have considered permitting such a fragmentation of our national effort, investment, and responsibility.

Some of our great national commitments, such as the T.V.A. and Hoover Dam, have had a regional focus, but most of the great causes that have united our country succeeded because they were national in scope, from the G.I. Bill of Rights to civil rights and from the Social Security of the New Deal to the collective security of NATO. A politics of scale is at work here, whereby the federal government is able to tackle formidable challenges more successfully than a state, not only because of its greater financial strength, but also, as James Madison foresaw, because of its greater ability to withstand and minimize the pressure of powerful special-interest groups opposed to the national interest.

What today's Republican politicians choose to ignore is that the same logic that applies to resistance against a foreign foe or to rescue efforts after a natural disaster applies with equal force to remedies for poverty and disease and hunger. Indeed, it was Republican President Nixon who declared hunger to be a serious national crisis, too clearly a federal responsibility to be left to individual states to solve. How ironic that the political party most upset over the "threat" posed by multiculturalism to our American national culture and English-language supremacy wishes to break up the Union into fifty or more pieces, some of which are bound to promote their own art, history, dialect, and food.

Once it was argued that the states governed best because they were closest to the people. Once. Unlike our Founding Fathers, I can now travel from New York City to Washington more easily than to Albany, and telephone or fax my congressman as quickly as my state assemblyman. Indeed, like most people, I can more readily name my congressman than my state representative, and am more likely to know how the former thinks and votes. (I certainly have no way of keeping track of or even identifying the literally thousands of separate but overlapping layers and levels of often inefficient and unaccountable local governments that over the centuries have gradually encrusted the tri-state region in which I live).

State and local governments already bear major responsibilities, not only for the municipal functions important to our daily lives, and not only as laboratories for small-scale experimentation on national issues that can lead to improved federal programs, but also as the local administrators of those programs. When the Republicans argue long and hard that most federal programs could be administered better at the state and local level than in Washington, D.C., it is well to remember that in fact they already are. Almost all federal programs with local impact are administered locally, either by local officers of the responsible federal agency or by state and local government offices dispensing federal or partly federal funds under federal guidelines. Less than one of every twelve federal civil servants works in the Washington area. But in the interest of uniformity and sanity—the sanity of both those who regulate and those who are regulated—a separate policy is not set by these local administrators for each state and local jurisdiction. On national problems where neither the states nor the private sector are able or willing to meet the nation's needs, the national government must set national policies and standards.

The question of state versus federal power is at heart not a legal issue. Despite conservative invocations of the Tenth Amendment statement of the obvious,* the constitutional power of Congress under Article I of the Constitution to "provide for the . . . general Welfare of the United States" and to "make all Laws which shall be necessary and proper" on any matter affecting more than one state, and the President's authority under Article II to take care that all such laws are "faithfully executed," leave little room for states to intrude uninvited into national problem areas already occupied by Congress.

Instead this is an issue of politics and power. The issue of the proper allocation of power between our national and state governments has been a fundamental dividing line in American politics since our earliest days: it exposed the inherent weaknesses of the Articles of Confederation; dominated the debates over the Constitution, the Bill of Rights, and the early establishment of a national bank; transformed the national moral and political struggle over slavery into an intensely bloody Civil War and bitter Reconstruction Period; and fueled the progressive reforms of the Industrial Age. The Democrats, founded on a Jeffersonian suspicion of centralized authority and on a Southern, originally slave-holding, political base, initially championed states' rights. Federalists like Alexander Hamilton, later followed by Republicans like Abraham Lincoln and Theodore Roosevelt, urged an increasingly stronger national government. States' rights in the Industrial Age, said T.R. to his fellow reformers, had become a "cover" for the "fight against government control and supervision

---

* "The powers not delegated to the United States by the Constitution, nor prohibited by it to the States, are reserved to the States respectively, or to the people."

of individual and corporate wealth engaged in interstate business."

Then, under the influence of the Great Depression and Franklin Roosevelt's New Deal, the two major parties switched sides. The Republicans and their business allies, unable to accept F.D.R.'s regulatory remedies and support for workers' rights, became the leading opponents of a strong national government. Democrats became its leading proponents. Southern states, welcoming federal government leadership when it meant Roosevelt's agricultural and regional development policies, overcame their unease with the big cities, labor unions, and other liberal members of the New Deal coalition to maintain their traditional Democratic moorings.

In the early days of the Depression, with state and local government credit collapsing and the use of federal authority inhibited by Republican conservatism, most American citizens experienced first hand the futility of trying to deal with a monumental nationwide economic crisis by means of the "widows' pensions," county poor farms, local orphanages, and other hopelessly inadequate tools of individual state and local governments. The federal government filled the vacuum because state and local governments could not handle it. With each economically pressed state hoping to attract new taxpayers (especially corporate taxpayers providing jobs) and hoping to discourage the inmigration of "tax-eaters," especially those needing food, shelter, and "relief," no single state was able or willing to adopt on its own the welfare, wage and hour, unemployment insurance, Social Security, and other programs by which Roosevelt's federal administration attacked the poverty and hopelessness of the Depression.

Similarly, in subsequent years, the tasks of assuring equal

rights and opportunities for all American citizens regardless of color, cleaning up the American environment, assuring minimum labor and safety standards, and a great many other fundamental national obligations could not be left solely to state and local governments. For economic as well as political reasons those governments were simply unwilling to promulgate costly or restrictive measures, however enlightened or necessary, unless similar measures were simultaneously promulgated by all the other states and localities with whom they were competing.

As earlier noted, some Democratic governors, during the years of Republican reign in the White House, did conduct admirable state-level demonstration projects on improvements in education, urban development, and other areas. But there is no evidence that the present majority of Republican governors—to whom the Republicans are now transferring unprecedented responsibility to deal with poverty, disease, pollution, occupational hazards, hunger, and myriad other national ailments, along with fewer dollars and fewer conditions—will be any more willing and able to attack these problems on a sustained basis, in good years and bad, any more capably and vigorously than were their predecessors in Franklin Roosevelt's time.

Nor is there any reason to believe that reshuffling these duties from regulation-prone federal bureaucracies to regulation-prone state bureaucracies offers any prospect for beneficial change. Apart from defense-related activities, the rapidly expanding state and local bureaucracies are today already larger and more expensive than their downsized federal counterparts. They enjoy no greater public confidence regarding either their efficiency or their effectiveness. State governments, which have mostly "balanced" their budgets (when state law so required) by borrowing the money needed for capital outlays and by raising regressive property and sales taxes, will not be any more likely in the coming years than they were in previous years to put their own funds into helping the unemployed, or even the slipping middle class—not if they can put those funds into more politically popular highways, golf courses, and sports arenas.

Freed from federal mandates, the states will be more inclined than ever to compete with one another in cutting those unpopular programs in a mean and stingy race to the bottom. States competing for business by beggaring their neighbors—keeping taxes, wages, environmental regulations, and labor union rights at the lowest possible levels—will surely attract some fly-by-night companies (before they fly off again to Thailand or Vietnam for still cheaper workers), but such states will not be serving our common national interests.

I would like to believe that all fifty of our state governments have become less inefficient, less retrograde, less penurious, racist, sexist, mean-spirited, and untrustworthy than in the past. But it is absurd to argue that either state bureaucracies or state legislatures in Albany, Sacramento, Baton Rouge, or any other state capital, still receiving less news coverage than Washington, are any "closer" in any meaningful way to the vast majority of their constituents than Washington legislators and administrators, or know the wishes of their constituents any better, or report to them any more fully, or are any less prone to engage in logrolling or pork-barreling, or are any less vulnerable to the pressures and temptations proffered by high-powered lobbyists.

The two Roosevelts, like Madison, both stressed the need for a strong national government to hold to public account the depredations and manipulations of strong national corporations and private interest organizations. The states cannot do it. Despite their devolutionary rhetoric, members of today's Republican

Congress, bent on parceling out federal programs to fifty state governments, know full well that it is turning power back not to "the people" but to those same powerful private interests (and, in the case of public schools, to right-wing religious interests). As the distinguished historian Arthur Schlesinger, Jr., has written, "Local government is the government of the locally powerful. Historically, it has been the national government that served as the protector of the powerless . . . against local exploitation or neglect."

In moving to turn still more policy as well as administration and financing over to the states, the Republicans took no notice of how well or poorly the states had handled other functions and funds previously delegated to them, under such measures as law enforcement assistance, the Model Cities program, urban redevelopment, tuberculosis prevention, and other past examples of devolution not noted for their efficiency and success once they were in state hands. Too often responsibilities were shirked, prior gains were lost, monies were squandered, and funds were diverted.

It has become increasingly clear to virtually everyone, including in their hearts most Republicans, that their party's single-minded "devolution revolution" is not intended primarily to reform or improve the programs devolved, because the states will be unable to do so. Nor is it intended to place the implementation of those programs at the state and local level, because it is mostly there already. Nor is it designed to increase efficiency or reduce red tape or build a new national consensus for or against these programs, because they will be scattered across fifty states. Nor is it intended to reverse the growth of government bureaucracy, because they have merely shifted these activities to a lower level.

Instead, the main objective is to conceal with the tiniest of fig leaves the federal abandonment of these responsibilities. The true Republican goal in 1995 was and remains a sharp reduction in the overall financing and coverage of these programs. In short, the real objective is deregulation, not devolution; decimation, not decentralization. A party genuinely committed to the principles of states' rights and responsibilities would not be undoing state health reforms, overruling state tort and product liability laws, mandating new state welfare eligibility requirements, and massively invading the area once traditionally and most decisively reserved for the exercise of state authority, law enforcement.

If, pursuant to this strategy, children cut off from federal assistance end up on the streets, if wetlands cut off from federal protection end up as swamps or sewage dumps, if poor schools cut off from federal funding end up producing mostly dependents and delinquents, the states will be blamed, not Congress. Accusations dispersed across fifty different states at different times in far-off, underreported state capitals will be more easily avoided by national leaders. State governments unwilling to take the bait and shirk these new responsibilities, and those too subject to close press scrutiny to do so even if they were willing, will simply be required to place themselves at a competitive disadvantage by coming up with funds not required in other states. The state governments that are willing to shirk these responsibilities will not be accountable to United States citizens outside those states' borders who are outraged that such inhumane malpractice in governance could occur within our country.

"Block grants" were the method repeatedly used by the new Republicans to achieve this devolution: consolidating existing federal activities, obligations, and commitments in each broad area of activity, combining them with numerous categorical grants into a single, limited lump sum with few or no strings attached, and handing the whole package off to the states. One scholar accurately described this practice as "kicking the problem down to the states to solve." Another called it a "secret device for cutting . . . benefits [while] avoiding blame."

In truth, this deceptively simple device is neither all new (Presidents Johnson and Nixon initiated many block grants, many of them failures) nor all bad (by 1994 hundreds of proliferating categorical grants had created a bureaucratic nightmare for the states). But block grants too often fail to allow for different quantities of demand on the states, different qualities of preparation and performance by the states, different rates of growth and prosperity in the states, different state costs of living, different levels of state effort, innovative state experiments, or the ever-present possibility of state government waste, fraud, and abuse.

Nor is a block grant a secure arrangement for either side of this bargain. No hard-pressed state, pressed still harder to meet its own vast new responsibilities under this approach, can count on a Congress bent on reducing the federal government's own deficit and taxes to provide additional funds for block-grant programs to which the state becomes committed. This will be especially true, and damaging, once demand rises in hard times when the state is least able to add its own funding. Nor can Congress be counted upon to refrain from continually adding new conditions in the future (as it has in the past) that turn a block grant back into a series of highly contingent, individual categorical grants. For its part, the federal government has reason to fear that too many states, receiving federal tax funds with few or no conditions, will feel less constrained to spend that money properly, much less to assure that grant's sufficiency by adding enough of their own locally raised funds.

Federal Aid to Dependent Children, the principal welfare assistance program, was a particularly callous choice for the Republican block grant maneuver. State governments, which had already been in the process of steadily reducing welfare spending and benefits for some years, can always find uses for their money that are politically more appealing, once relieved of the requirement to contribute any specified level of their own funds for poor children. The struggle to fund social programs will be particularly fierce once mandated workfare requirements—which experience indicates can cost far more than they save—exhaust the federal grant. The competition in each state legislature for a share of inadequate block grants will be a sad spectacle. With no more national floor, no more federal commitment to a child's decent existence, the way has been paved for an ugly change in the very heart and soul of America.

As demonstrated by Vice President Gore's "reinventing government" proposals, the Democratic Party, which pioneered state and local government participation in the administration of federal programs and grants and which has often been a leader in devising new creative approaches to poverty and education at the state level, does not favor a monopoly of power at the federal level. Democrats know that further decentralization and dispersion would be consistent with many of the economic and technological trends of the post-industrial era: one leading voice, one policy, but many participants. *Pluribus* is still important to *unum*.

But the globalization of commerce and the increased centralization in the ownership of the media and other economic interests makes all the more important a single strong national economic policy promoting growth and opportunity, and makes all the more unviable the notion of fifty state governments competing on their own against one another. If professional sports franchise owners can play one American state and city off against another in full public view, consider what major multinational companies will be doing beyond our purview. When the next national or global recession affects the fifty states unevenly, as it always has and will, the cry for reviving federal help, coordination, and compensation could be deafening.

In short, the federal government should not now be abandoning its responsibility to set basic policy and standards on national issues. It should not be abandoning its obligation to assure a minimum safety net under every citizen, regardless of local politics or prejudice. In place of block grants and out of-control devolution, a Democratic Congress and President should do the following:

- Consolidate more categorical grants and the separate forms and reports they entail, and remove petty and redundant regulations that irritate and exacerbate state agencies.
- Expand the use of waivers to give more states more flexibility to serve as laboratories of public policy, and give states more leeway to design and operate their own plans for implementing federal policy.
- Rely more on challenge grants that reward improved quality of performance, measured not by increases in numbers of beneficiaries but by increases in job placements and other concrete results.
- Send more decision-making and financial authority to the ultimate recipient, whether a city, a school, or even an individual, who could be given a voucher to choose and fund his or her placement in a worthwhile job, training program, or residence.
- Try wider use of the contractual approach, pioneered by

Oregon, in which federal, state, and local governments agree on benchmarks that the federal government will fund as the state and local governments fulfill them. This gives the latter wide latitude on how to achieve those benchmarks—in short, state flexibility combined with accountability, making possible federal devolution of operations without abandonment of obligations.

Even with these reforms, the distribution of power between federal and state governments will no doubt continue to be debated. The dividing line will no doubt move back and forth from time to time, depending on circumstances as well as politics. Clearly, though, the Republican rush to abdicate national responsibilities to the states today threatens our national strength and cohesion at the worst possible time. We face a difficult period of intense domestic social tensions, international economic competition, and increasingly aggressive encroachments on public interest concerns by nationally and internationally powerful private interests. Emasculating the authority of the federal government undermines the strength of the one American institution best equipped to meet those challenges.

This is no time to splinter the American economy into fifty separate economies and virtually redefine the meaning and obligations of being an American. It is a time to be looking out for our fellow Americans in every state. It is a time for shared responsibility, to meet the obligations of community—the national community of which we are all members. Those obligations and the national values that underlie them cannot be devolved.

It is a time for united leadership under a party that believes in strong national leadership. That party is the Democratic Party, and that is another reason why I am a Democrat.

# ☆ CHAPTER 9 ☆
## UPHOLDING THE LAW
☆ ☆ ☆

*I am committed to the rule of law and order in our society.* That commitment reflects my professional obligation as well as my personal philosophy as a long-time practicing lawyer and thus an officer of the court. As the son, brother, and father of lawyers, all of whom had prosecutorial experience, and the loving friend of two great leaders gunned down in the midst of their political careers, I abhor all crime, whether on the streets or in executive suites. I do not favor the "coddling" of any criminals, rich or poor, black or white, young or old. Nor do I favor the legalization of mind-altering drugs that destroy the will and reason of our citizens. When crimes large and small go unpunished, or when a guilty criminal goes free, or when a released repeat offender strikes again, I am filled with rage like all law-abiding citizens. Given the unacceptably high crime rate in this country, and the public's insistence that the federal government do something about it, I was not surprised that the Republicans nationalized this previously local issue in the 1964 and 1968 elections.

But the prevention of crime is one of those issues that has no uniquely Republican or Democratic solution. It does not and should not divide the parties philosophically. Neither party is soft on crime or criminals, various campaign "attack" commercials to the contrary notwithstanding. Lawmakers who are also lawbreakers have disgraced themselves in both parties. The families and constituencies of Republicans and Democrats alike, liberals and conservatives, are equally fearful of and vulnerable to crime. The poor and middle class, prime Democratic Party constituencies, are victimized the most.

Black and Hispanic families and neighborhoods suffer more from violent crime than anyone else, and their leaders are the first to say that neither poverty nor discrimination is an excuse for criminal conduct. Although it is an unfortunate fact that racism persists in the hearts of all kinds of Americans, including many law enforcement officers and jury members, and that the Republican Party has sought to turn crime into a race issue in the political arena, there is nothing racist about favoring more effective curbs on crime, and there is nothing illiberal about enacting measures that effectively enhance the security of all neighborhoods. Unfortunately, neither party is certain what those measures are, particularly at the federal level.

Build more prisons? Governors and Presidents from both parties have invested enormous sums in establishing more and more prisons to serve the world's highest rate of incarceration, except for Russia's. Yet neither those incarcerations nor those prisons have prevented a violent-crime rate that is also many times higher than that in most other nations.

Halt drug use? Both political parties have deplored the widespread use of drugs and the amount of crime stemming from drug abuse. Thus far, however, the interdiction of foreign drug imports has been too difficult to succeed, the long-term rehabilitation of addicts has been too expensive to succeed, and preventive education has been too slow and its success remains uncertain.

Increase punishment? Each of the major parties is internally divided on capital punishment as a moral issue, and neither side of that debate has any definitive evidence as to whether the presence or absence of that option significantly deters or encourages either murders or convictions. But that has not discouraged Republicans in Washington from adding more and more items to the list of federal crimes incurring the death penalty, knowing full well that no colleague will dare oppose a popular measure that carries an anticrime label or even question why we constantly need new congressional legislation burdening state and local officials, or interfering with or taking over more and more law enforcement decisions and functions once left largely to them. On this issue, all praise and pledges for the principles of "devolution" are forgotten.

Politics, polls, and public concern have pushed crime onto the congressional agenda, and both parties now compete to see whose proposals can be toughest, if not necessarily wisest or most effective. If one party one year favors more police on the streets, then the other favors curfews and longer sentences. If one house of Congress emphasizes shortening criminal trials and the appeals process, the other emphasizes safer schoolyards and housing projects. If the party in power takes one route, the opposition takes the other. Opportunities to switch proposals are plentiful, inasmuch as a new crime bill has been enacted every few years during the last decade or more, usually as election time nears.

Over that same period, the crime rate among juveniles has risen 100 percent.

Despite these philosophical similarities, two major differences divide the parties on this issue. The first is the Democrats' willingness to identify and address not only crime and all its symptoms and consequences but also its causes and conditions. That approach is more complex and costly, and less suited to bumper stickers and applause lines, but it is also more honest. Although criminal behavior is not unknown among families in nice neighborhoods with good schools, it is no secret that there is more crime where poverty and unemployment abound, where desperation and hopelessness prevail, where respect among young school dropouts for our laws and even our lives is greatly diminished.

I have previously emphasized that deprivation and discrimination do not excuse criminal offenses by any individual. But Republican opposition to the urban health, housing, job-training, and education programs that could make a difference is also inexcusable. So is their opposition to those measures that would help keep more young people in school and enable the best of them to attend college, that would help reduce the rate of child abuse and illiteracy that twist young minds, and that would help end racial discrimination in education, employment, and housing.

Republican legislators have called the inner city a "breeding place of crime," as the shocking statistics demonstrate. Blacks are more likely than whites to be victims of murder and most other crimes in this country. There are more black men in jail than in college—indeed, almost one in three black men in their twenties is either in jail, on parole, or on probation. But those inner cities will continue to breed crime and criminals at a disproportionate rate under Republican proposals to cut back on aid to disadvantaged schools, on funds to house the poor, on Medicaid, affirmative action, and all the other Democratic programs that would offer a life of greater opportunity and options to all Americans.

The Republican Party's answer to these conditions, in the words of one of its most articulate leaders, William Bennett, is to "blow up the welfare system, [and] abolish the Department of Education, the National Endowments and Public Broadcasting." (Now there's a solution to the crime problem.) The Republicans have demagogued the crime issue for years. But it is the Democratic Party, not the Republican Party, that is entitled to borrow a plank from the platform of the resurgent British Labour Party: "Tough on crime, *and* tough on the causes of crime."

The second major point of divergence between the parties on the question of crime is gun control. The term "control" is itself a gross exaggeration. The Democrats finally enacted, and the Republicans upon achieving majority status promptly undertook to repeal, two small steps toward moderating the indiscriminate and massive sale, ownership, and often violent use of guns in this country. The first was the Brady Bill, which requires a five-day waiting period to check the background of each gun purchaser. The law prevented the purchase of tens of thousands of handguns by convicted felons and fugitives in its first year. The second measure was a ban on fifteen types of assault weapons suited not to hunting, target shooting, or even self-defense but to killing or maiming the most people in the least amount of time. Compared with the sweeping restrictions on the private ownership of weapons, particularly handguns, in virtually every other democracy on earth, these two steps were minuscule in a country with more than 200 million guns floating around.

Our police officers are required to walk the streets and charge into crime scenes knowing that they are likely to be overwhelmingly outgunned. Our children are being gunned down, often by other children, at a sharply increasing rate that has reached the incredible level of fifteen such incidents per day. More Americans are killed by guns—in murders, suicides, accidents, and otherwise—every eighteen months than the approximately 47,000 who died in the Vietnam War. Guns are used in seven out of every ten murders. Suicidal teenagers and younger children, addicts and wife abusers, convicted felons and lawbreakers awaiting trial—and, lest we forget, those who want to kill Presidents or pop stars, judges or doctors—all seem to have easy access to guns. Yet the Republican Party wants to repeal even these minimal ownership requirements.

The Republicans are also opposed to a ban on "cop-killer" bullets designed to rip through a supposedly bullet-proof vest. Why? Not to preserve the rights and fun of hunters. My son hunts deer near his home in northern Wisconsin. He does not believe that anyone should have an unregulated right to buy a handgun, much less an assault weapon, without restrictions or delays. In the words of President Clinton, my son has "never seen a deer, a duck or a wild turkey wearing a . . . [bullet-proof] vest."

Nor is the Republican position, contrary to some far-fetched claims, based on the Second Amendment to the Constitution, which preserves the right of state-regulated militias (now the National Guard) to bear arms. No federal court has ever struck down on Second Amendment grounds any legislative restriction on the private ownership or use of guns. No court has ever found any provision in the Constitution that either prohibits such restrictive legislation or permits gun ownership and use. I only wish those concerned about what they incorrectly see as the trampling of the Second Amendment were equally concerned about the attempted trampling of the First and Fifth amendments and other key provisions of the Constitution.

Republican Party opposition to any limitation on the private arsenal confronting America's police officers every day stems not from that party's concern for the United States Constitution or sportsmen but from its unholy alliance with the National Rifle Association (N.R.A.), the single-issue lobbying group known for its extremist views, its large campaign contributions, and its association with the fanatical fringe groups who constantly disparage and threaten federal law enforcement officers. Speaker Gingrich even sent a confidential letter to the N.R.A. pledging no more gun control legislation.

"[Y]ou can see who is in control" of the legislative branch, said President Clinton last year, when "this Congress is investigating the A.A.R.P. [American Association of Retired Persons] and letting the N.R.A. run one of [Congress's] own investigations," which was attempting to paint as villains the F.B.I. and the Alcohol, Tobacco, and Firearms Bureau.

Please do not tell me that "guns don't kill people, only people kill people." Without guns, Oswald could not have killed John Kennedy, Sirhan could not have killed Robert Kennedy, John Hinckley could not have wounded Ronald Reagan, James Earl Ray could not have killed Martin Luther King, Jr., and thousands upon thousands of other Americans could not have been killed by their murderers.

How strange that Republican leaders, like Bob Dole, condemn song lyrics that glorify the fictional killing of policemen, but do not condemn the availability of real guns that actually kill real policemen. How different it must be to work as a policeman or government leader or plain citizen in Japan, where private hand-guns are banned with severe penalties, a country with roughly one half our population that has fewer firearm murders in one year than we average in one day. The Republican Party's rejection of any limits on the availability of murder weapons in this country exposes the hollowness of its cynical crusade for law and order.

There is more to it than that. As a lawyer, my reverence for the rule of law in our society includes a reverence for our Constitution, that farsighted, brilliantly crafted charter of our basic governmental structure and principles, which since the original Bill of Rights was added soon after its enactment has required only seventeen Amendments in more than two hundred years. It is not a partisan document embodying any particular economic theory, any party's political agenda, or any specific legislative directions. It is instead a lean, flexible repository of our sovereignty, our highest expression of fundamental law, ideologically neither liberal nor conservative.

The new Republican zealots who took over the House of Representatives last year, however, taking great pride in reminding us all that they are *not* lawyers, have seemed at times to look upon the Constitution as just another piece of paper waiting to be remolded to their current political mood. In an unprecedented push to change this hallowed document, they introduced more than seventy new amendments during their first few months in office. At least three of these measures were quickly rushed through committee without ample time to consider with care their long-term consequences or the extent to which their wording was consistent with the work of the original Framers. These Republican legislators were trivializing the Constitution as if it were "a rough draft" (the words of Congresswoman Pat Schroeder)—or, as other commentators put it, "just another sound bite" or just "another implement in the lawmaker's toolbox to fix life's everyday problems."

No one questions the Republicans' right to pursue their political and legislative goals. But they should pursue them through the normal political and legislative processes, and not clutter up and politicize our nation's permanent charter. The legislative package of any particular Congress, reflecting the political whims and passions of the day, should be subject to modification or repeal in a later Congress, if opinions change or passions cool, and not be permanently locked into our basic legal structure. A Constitution designed, among other things, to preserve for all time the rights of political and other minorities against the "tyranny of the majority" should not and must not be changed every time a new majority is elected to office.

Should liberals, when they get the upper political hand, not only undertake to repeal Republicans' constitutional amendments but also insert a few of their own, perhaps adding specific social and economic entitlements to the Bill of Rights, as many other countries have done, or broadening the ban on governmental interference with free speech and assembly to cover private interference as well? They should not, and I hope that they would not. Comity, continuity, and confidence in this country require what constitutional scholar Kathleen Sullivan has called a clear "boundary between law and politics. The more you amend the Constitution, the more it seems like ordinary legislation . . . [and] the less it looks like a fundamental charter of government."

The principal amendments that the Republicans last year tried to bull through the Congress for ratification by the states all illustrate the dangers of a new temporary congressional majority's trying to use the Constitution, instead of legislation, to work its will.

1. *Term Limits for Members of Congress.* This concept, which was contained in the discredited Articles of Confederation, was rejected by the Constitutional Convention because it would deny voters the right to choose the most experienced candidates. It became a highly popular idea at the beginning of this understandably disillusioned decade. But, even for Republicans, the idea sounded a lot better before their own Party took over both Houses of Congress and discovered that new, inexperienced legislators are much more dependent than were their veteran predecessors on those previously despised bureaucrats, lobbyists, and permanent Hill staff members. Some of today's freshmen Republicans may even decide, after all, to become tomorrow's "career politicians." Whether they do or not, the voters are free now to limit through the ballot box the number of terms served by any Congressman not representing their interests; and they have done so, and will continue to do so, without any need to amend the Constitution.

2. *Mandatory Balanced Budget Amendment.* This proposal, which came within one vote of passing the Senate, was in effect a congressional plea to "stop me before I overspend again." The stated objective was to require a balanced budget every year, re-

gardless of economic conditions. The real objective
was to block forever any new programs, regardless
of merit, and to emasculate all the old programs
opposed by the current conservative Republican
orthodoxy. The strategy was to make that straight-
jacket permanent as quickly as possible, while this
limited, penurious view of government is still popular, and without being required to disclose to current voters the amendment's inevitably adverse
effects on Medicare, education, and other popular
and essential programs.

Because its wording and implications had not
been carefully thought through, this amendment
bogged down in floor arguments over precisely
what it covered, and what powers the courts would
have if Congress ever enacted an "unconstitu-
tional" budget.

In addition, the amendment as proposed required super-majority votes in both houses of Congress for every proposed increase in the deficit, the
debt limit, or taxes. That would enable a minority
in either house to paralyze the entire government
by blocking virtually any and every bill, no matter
how urgent, merited, or desired by the people and
by both houses. The Constitution now requires
congressional super-majorities only for extraordinary actions, such as convicting an impeached
President, ousting a wayward member of Congress,
overriding a presidential veto, approving treaties,
and proposing constitutional amendments. Our

Founding Fathers explicitly rejected the notion that power over ordinary legislation should "be transferred to the minority," as Madison put it.

3. *The Flag Desecration Amendment.* This amendment would for the first time in our history alter the Bill of Rights and First Amendment, with their free-speech guarantees. To what purpose? In order to overturn a sound and courageous United States Supreme Court decision and authorize punishment of the five or six fanatics per year who seek attention by burning or ridiculing or in some other way abusing our national symbol. Because the flag in today's world is so often used in myriad ways, some of them nutty or smutty, on clothes and in shows, in songs and in art, the possibilities for zealous bureaucrats or judges to stretch to ridiculous lengths this ban on offensive, provocative but heretofore free expression are obvious. What is not obvious is what large constitutional concern requires this change. True, it offers the Republicans an easy vote and a grand applause line on Flag Day and Independence Day, but surely purely symbolic patriotism does not by itself honor the flag.

In fact, there are many ways by which elected officials can and do dishonor the American flag and the basic principles for which it stands—but their only punishment, often avoided, is electoral defeat.

4. *The Religious Equality Amendment.* There are two competing versions of such an amendment being pushed by competing Republican factions, and

both would also fundamentally alter the First Amendment. Each would devise rationales to permit denominational preaching, prayers, and other forms of organized religious activity in schools and other public facilities supported by taxpayers of all (and no) denominations. Both proposals could lead to taxpayer support of parochial schools. Such an amendment would reopen the door to all the sectarian tensions and fears that many of our forebears fled Europe to escape and the Framers sought to avoid by insisting on a strict separation of church and state. Any student can pray in school now, as noted in the next chapter; clarification of that right does not require or justify a far-reaching amendment to the Constitution.

The school prayer, flag-burning, abortion, and many of the other current political controversies that the Republicans want to fix for all time by changing our national charter have arisen as the result of U.S. Supreme Court decisions unwelcome to them. Because the Court's role is to decide what is lawful and constitutional, not what is popular, its decisions often displease the majority. Rushing in to amend the Constitution each time that happens would destroy the national sense of final resolution that gives the Court much of its institutional weight and respect.

I say that with conviction, notwithstanding my political foreboding over the growing sway held by Reagan-Bush appointees on the High Court, conservative activists whose numbers and power could grow further under a right-wing presidency. Undecided or unenthusiastic voters must keep this eventuality in mind.

Another vital source of the judiciary's public esteem and hence its independence has long been its accessibility to all, regardless of status or wealth. I am thus deeply troubled by the erosion of this principle of equal justice threatened by a series of new Republican measures to restrict the access of "little people" to the courts and to legal representation, and to restrict their effective ability to obtain redress for wrongs done to them. Leading Republican officeholders seem ready to regard the law almost as a nuisance, as an impediment, an irritant that should be ignored or sidestepped. Some of the more recent reckless legislative objectives of the Gingrich-Dole era include the following:

- In the name of "tort reform," make it more difficult for persons of modest means, when bilked by a fraudulent securities firm or when permanently impaired by a malpracticing physician, by the product of a careless toy manufacturer, by a drunken driver, or by an egregious polluter, to recover the level of damages necessary to compensate those persons fairly and enable them to retain expert legal counsel.
- Intimidate ordinary citizens and scare them away from suing large companies—which can afford to prolong expensive trials indefinitely—by requiring those individual plaintiffs to pay the legal fees for both sides if they lose.
- Dismantle the Legal Services Corporation, a Nixon-era agency that for over twenty years has provided free legal representation to poor women seeking to escape abusive husbands, migrant workers cheated out of their menial pay, welfare recipients unlawfully evicted from their apartments, and other victims of fraud, discrimination, and injustice who could not afford legal counsel. In addi-

tion, legislation proposed by Republicans would forbid those upstart Legal Services Corporation lawyers from ever challenging any government or welfare agency decision or rule, advising any legislative committee, representing any class of plaintiffs, counseling any client about divorce (a clause inserted by the Christian Coalition), representing any migrant workers (because the Farm Bureau lobby said most such complaints were for "only small amounts of wages") . . . the list goes on.

- Finally, halt the provision of legal counsel, and limit the right to federal habeas corpus, for death row inmates who may have been unjustly convicted or sentenced.

As a lawyer I am deeply offended by these Republican moves. Not because I am either a "bleeding-heart" or a litigator whose income could be affected, for I am neither, not because I deny or defend the obvious shortcomings that exist today in the legal profession in our overly litigious society, for I do not. I am offended because I believe in the motto "equal justice under law." The right to legal counsel is so imbedded in our heritage that its provision is the *only* right to professional assistance contained in our Constitution. It is not only cruel, it is dangerous to tell large numbers of people who believe they have been denied a fair shake that they cannot obtain redress through our legal system, i.e., they must obtain it outside the legal system or not at all.

"They talk to you like you are dumb," a reporter was told by a woman in Savannah whose daughter needed a Legal Services lawyer to assert her clearly justified claim against her landlord. "When you have a lawyer, they talk to you like you are a person." Democrats want all U.S. citizens treated like they are persons. As a believer in the rule of law, I am a Democrat.

# ☆ CHAPTER 10 ☆
## PRESERVING THE FAMILY
☆ ☆ ☆

*I am a family man with a conservative life-style.* I deeply love my wife of twenty-seven years, I love my four children and my four grandchildren, and I strongly believe that the integrity and happiness of the family are pillars of our society's health and cohesion. I will always be grateful to my late parents for my strict upbringing, permitting no alcohol or cigarettes, no profanity or pornography, and no tendencies toward violence or indolence. Having attended a conservative college and law school, neither my tastes in clothes, hairstyle, literature, or music—nor my lifetime habits at home and at work—could ever be deemed, even by Newt Gingrich, to reflect what he calls the "counterculture" or "alternative life-styles." I am disgusted by the sleaze and violence that characterize so much of this nation's entertainment and advertising today, and I have no interest in exhibitions billed as "performance art" that in my view contain very little of either. I have tried to teach my children that individual and family responsibility is more important than instant gratification, and I have long believed that a moral foundation should exist for every major public policy position, because a nation's greatness cannot ultimately be separated from its goodness.

None of that makes me either a unique and lonely Democrat or a Republican. Nor does it cause me to feel that the Republicans have an edge on the Democrats in any political debate over family values and moral issues. Neither political party has a monopoly on those issues, or favors a "values-free" government. Both parties recognize the urgent need to protect and strengthen the family and its enduring role and values in our society. Both parties recognize the benefits to a child of having both parents in the home (although a quarter of America's children do not), and both parties have supported measures against "deadbeat dads" who economically abandon mother and child. Both parties deplore the tragic rise of divorce, desertion, and unwed—often teenage— motherhood, which, while increasing in all Western democracies, make up a disturbing 30 percent or more of U.S. births. Unfortunately, this trend—along with the increased number of those who prefer to remain childless, remarry, or live alone—has sharply diminished in this country the proportion of traditional nuclear family units composed of children and their two married parents.

Both political parties equally deplore abuse of women and children, violence in the home, school, and neighborhood, and the deterioration of conditions and learning in too many public schools. Both equally deplore the spread of AIDS, illicit drugs, and hard-core pornography, particularly when involving or accessible to children. Both favor priority for parents in directing the upbringing of their children. (No new law is needed for this, the U.S. Supreme Court having recognized that priority under the Constitution long ago). Both favor the instillation in all Americans of a greater sense of individual responsibility and community.

Neither party is free to cast the first stone at divorced or sexually wayward politicians in the other party, or to make political hay out of either the peaking in the number of births to teenagers during one party's administration (Eisenhower's) or in the number of families headed by women alone during the other party's administration (Clinton's). The adherents of both parties include the devoutly religious, the ostensibly religious, the occasionally religious, and the nonreligious, none of whom possesses all of the Truth or produces only perfect children. Despite some Republican claims to the contrary, God, to the best of my knowledge, is not a registered member of either party.

But none of this has deterred the Republican leaders and their religious-right backers from adopting a self-righteous, holier-than-thou attitude on this subject, insisting that they are morally superior to the Democrats, that their values and beliefs are the only acceptable values and beliefs, and that their control of Congress gives them the right to impose these values and beliefs on the rest of the country, imposing them especially on the poor and downtrodden. (Presumably, they would exempt from their strictures some of the more prominent sinners among the televangelists and politicians in their own ranks.)

Democrats, remembering the massive and damaging failure of Prohibition to legislate a lasting change of one aspect of the population's behavior, are not so enamored of promoting the federal government to the role of national morals policeman and judge. The inculcation of positive values and motivations, while most important, is better left first to the family, and then to local religious, educational, neighborhood, and community institutions, each in its own appropriate sphere of activity. The federal government can help encourage and strengthen local community activities, but Democrats believe its regulatory authority and financial resources can best strengthen and protect the family if effectively used to address the daunting economic problems that are straining poor and middle-class American families today. These problems help break up families, erode their hopes, distort their values, and remove their stake in an orderly society.

Senator Dole has stated that problems like violence and unwed motherhood are solely questions of character, not economics. Certainly our national character—including the compassion, self-lessness, and determination of our people, as well as their morality—is being tested by these new social strains, but so is our approach to economics. The growth and strength of traditional middle-class values depend first and foremost on the growth and strength of the middle class itself. Middle-class families are now reeling from the pressures of income stagnation and inegalitarianism. The conclusions of repeated studies are clear:

- Communities with rising incomes and ample jobs have sturdier families, healthier children, better schools, fewer drugs, less crime, and more stability.
- Communities with fewer jobs, increasing unemployment, and lower, declining wages have more child and spousal abuse, more children born out of wedlock, more alcohol and drug abuse, and more crime and broken homes.
- In the absence of day-care programs, the unsupervised children of mothers forced to work longer hours because of declining family income are more likely to get into trouble.

- Teenagers who drop out of poorly staffed and funded schools, who have neither the money to attend college nor the skills to obtain jobs, and thus little hope for the future, are more likely (in the case of girls) to become pregnant out of wedlock and (in the case of boys) to turn to drugs or crime. By contrast, those who complete their education or job training with long-term confidence in the future and in themselves are more likely to find work, to get married, to serve as role models and counselors for others, and to participate in community and church activities.

In short, the best way to strengthen America's family values is to restore the American dream as the realistic goal of every American family. In this context the Democrats have long taken the lead, seeking to strengthen family values through policies designed to create more long-term employment opportunities and more public investment in people and technology. The emphasis has been on family opportunity and security:

- Opportunity and security for the working poor, through a higher minimum wage and restoration of the full earned-income tax credit (called "the best pro-family . . . measure to come out of Congress" by Ronald Reagan).
- Opportunity and security for working mothers, through affirmative action, affordable child-care facilities, and the family and child leave law.
- Opportunity and security for both husbands and wives in the workforce, through revised occupational health and safety standards, job training and retraining pro-

grams, portable pensions, and expanded health insurance.

- Opportunity and security for their aged parents, through Social Security, Medicare, and both home care and nursing home care under Medicaid, without the patient's spouse and adult children being required to first exhaust their own savings and other assets, and without their needing to fear such past (federally unregulated) nursing home practices as insufficient beds, dog food for dinner, and excessive reliance on sedation and physical restraints.

- Opportunity and security for their children, through an expanded Head Start program that offers school lunch and inoculations as well as education, summer jobs for kids, better schools, and more low-interest student loans that can bring a college degree—increasingly indispensable and increasingly expensive—within reach. In the first twenty-five years of Head Start, far fewer of its graduates later became high school dropouts, teenage mothers, or criminal gang members when compared to their non–Head Start peers.

Strains on typical middle-class families are caused less by downtown peep shows than by unpaid medical bills, unaffordable college tuitions, unavailable child-care facilities, and layoffs by downsized companies looking for a different kind of skill. A poor family, particularly in an economy offering fewer jobs for the unskilled, faces these strains and more—when there is not enough money left from a dwindling welfare or unemployment check to hold out until the next job can be found, or to pay for the children's lunch at school, or even to pay the daily bus or subway fare to a new job. For both the poor and middle class, family integrity and stability require family planning, including access to safe and reliable contraceptive information, methods, and services to prevent unwanted and unaffordable pregnancies.

Most of all, in an era of rising requirements and falling income, families need access to good, secure jobs, meaning better wages, schooling, training, and health and child care. It also means we need the kind of research and development in science and technology that create new and better jobs. Restoring faith in the old work ethic—that if you work hard enough, you will get ahead—is, as Secretary of Labor Robert Reich has said, "the moral core at the center of capitalism."

If "pro-family" has become the new political password, as the Republicans indicate, then Democrats have been "pro-family" for at least sixty years, proposing and enacting legislation for Social Security and low-cost housing credits, Medicare and Medicaid, Head Start and student loans, legal services and job training, the minimum wage and the EITC, programs that have done more to keep American families together and upwardly mobile over the years than any amount of Republican moralizing ever could. Yet the Republicans opposed these programs. When the household's breadwinner dies American families depend more upon Social Security for life insurance than on all private insurance companies combined. Without Social Security, roughly half of our elderly citizens would be living below the poverty line. That may not fit the Republican definition of "individual responsibility," but it is certainly "pro-family."

The Republican Party's "pro-family" program does not offer much by way of relieving the chronic job and wage anxiety now afflicting the lives of most middle-class American families, both parents and children. It offers more pain and castigation than

hope and help to most families headed by women, blacks, Hispanics, immigrants, welfare recipients, or people outside the old-
fashioned nuclear mold. True, they favored a $500 per child
"family" nonrefundable tax credit, but it benefited primarily those
in the upper tax brackets who could take full advantage of it.
True, they favored capital gains and other tax breaks for those
families who don't need an economic boost, but how much of
that would ultimately "trickle down" to the rest of society?

The Republicans' principal contribution to the security of poor
and middle-class families has been to "liberate" them from government's corrupting influence and interference by blocking or
cutting back all the Democratic programs mentioned earlier in
this chapter, from Medicare to school lunches to federal funding
and regulations for nursing homes. The moral fiber of too many
American families, the Republicans argue, has been crippled by
their dependence on such programs as a "crutch." The Republican solution is to kick away the crutch.

Alvin and Heidi Toffler, Mr. Gingrich's favorite futurists, have
said that it is "both necessary and morally right to provide [to the
unemployed] decent levels of public assistance." But Mr. Gingrich and his followers apparently believe instead that poverty is a
matter of choice, that anyone can find a sufficiently well-paying
job to climb out of poverty, regardless of education, training,
health, location, age, race, and obligations to dependents. In their
eyes, too much compassion, not too little, especially compassion
without enough strings attached to it, has been the problem, and
cannot now be part of the solution.

Having repudiated in last year's welfare "reform" bill our society's obligation to the poor, the Republican Party prefers instead
to lecture the poor on their obligations to society. Exhorting
almost 40 million Americans who live in poverty to find jobs may

be well-intended. But half of them are already in worker-headed households anyway. Without adequate minimum wages, job retraining opportunities, and earned-income tax credits, a job may not be enough these days to get out of poverty. Why did these Republican moralizers, nearly all male, cut funds for day care and after-class school activities? And why did they eviscerate the relatively new and formerly bipartisan Violence Against Women Act, slashing its funding for battered women's shelters, rape crisis centers, victims' assistance programs, and training for those enforcing these laws? Why have they reduced funds for drug treatment and rehabilitation?

Subjecting the one out of thirteen welfare mothers who is a teenager to punishment by cutting off her payments—or educational assistance— has not been shown to reduce pregnancies, much less poverty or the need for public assistance. Nor, contrary to myth, has it been shown that states with higher welfare payments face higher rates of welfare-mother pregnancy. Is it "pro-family" to punish innocent children for choosing parents who fail to marry, or fail to avoid pregnancy, or fail to find work? Inasmuch as rates of unwed motherhood have risen mostly among white women who are neither teenagers nor on welfare, it appears that this trend, both in this increasingly rootless and restless country and abroad, reflects primarily not the "welfare state" that the Republicans like to blame but larger, long-term changes in mores, including the feminist, information, and sexual revolutions, which governments cannot easily reverse.

But the Republican Party is bent on reversal. Already turning back the clock to stigmatize, penalize, and discriminate against children born out of wedlock or gay, the party has been committed by its religious right wing to further pursue, into the privacy of the bedroom and the obstetrician's office, Americans whose personal practices may not conform to those of the self-anointed guardians of the nation's moral conduct. For many years the Republican Party has consistently and persistently sought to outlaw by constitutional amendment a woman's right to freely choose, with her own doctor, mate, or clergy, whether to have an abortion. It seeks to criminalize that right when possible, to prevent the use of federal funds or facilities for abortions in the military or under Medicaid, and to minimize or exclude any exemptions for pregnancies resulting from rape or incest or even when the mother's life is at stake. Perhaps in some savage world of ethnic cleansing a woman can be forced to bear her rapist's baby—but in the United States of America?

Whether or when abortion is a woman's constitutional right or a murderous act depends upon the different question of when a fetus becomes an independently viable "person." The nation's best legal and scientific minds have determined the answers to both questions carefully and conclusively. Before the Supreme Court's decision legalizing abortion operations, it should be remembered, many American women desperate to terminate their pregnancies did so. A woman with sufficient means found her way to an offshore jurisdiction or to a doctor willing to certify that her life would be endangered. Those who lacked the necessary money and information resorted to self-mutilation, amateurs, outlaws, and back-alley operations that often ended in death, permanent disfigurement, or inability to bear further children.

Democrats are pro-choice, not mindlessly pro-abortion. They do not favor the use of abortion for routine birth control or for offspring gender selection purposes. Nor do they favor carelessly postponing that operation to so late in a woman's pregnancy that the rarely used "partial birth" method of abortion is required.

They do not discourage the adoption alternative when freely chosen, and would like it to be made a much easier, more viable alternative.

Democrats at all levels of government also oppose measures advocated by Republicans that are certain to increase the number of unwanted pregnancies terminated by abortion—such as defunding the family planning and contraception education services offered by Planned Parenthood and Medicaid clinics, prohibiting the teaching of sex education (including methods of avoiding pregnancy as well as sexually transmitted disease) in public high school health courses, and warning the pregnant mother on welfare that the birth of another child means an end to the stipend on which she lives. Conversely, they fear that the Republican determination to prevent the Medicaid funding of abortions for women on welfare means more teenagers giving birth and even more mothers and children less likely to escape welfare.

Abortion is not the only or the most important family issue to most Democrats. But they know that a woman's freedom of choice is an issue that cannot be ignored or referred back to the states, or made to disappear, as many Republicans wish. And it will not disappear so long as that party continues its effort to deny the fundamental right of all women, recognized in the declaration of the 1995 World Women's Conference in Beijing, to exercise control over their own sexuality, free of coercion, discrimination, violence, and abuse, both in the home and outside it.

Delegates from all nations, faiths, and backgrounds debated that provision with civility and mutual respect. How sad that those qualities cannot characterize the debate on abortion in this country, both in and out of Congress. How sad that fanatics of the religious right assume that the exercise of a woman's constitutional right can be halted by coercive demonstrations, intimidation, tear gas, the murder of medical practitioners, and the firebombing of medical clinics. They target both privately operated clinics and those operated by Planned Parenthood and other like-minded organizations, whose work on family planning represents the nation's best hope to reduce the rate of abortion. One of the Planned Parenthood clinics subjected to that kind of vicious attack was named for my wife's deceased parents, two lifelong faithful Republicans.

The Republicans like to call these intrusions into Americans' private lives and personal freedoms "cultural issues." They urge middle-class voters whom they are hurting on economic issues to join their party on the righteous path of these "cultural issues." They promise the Christian Coalition that, in exchange for its support on economic measures that are contrary to the wishes and best interests of many middle-class Coalition members, it will be assured in return of the Republican Party's support on "cultural issues."

This hubristic moralizing and meddling is not my idea of culture. I am more interested in the cultural fare on public broadcasting, providing relief from the dumb and dumber, vulgar and violence-filled shows on commercial television—and yet, strangely, it was public television and radio that the Republicans decided to shut down. Of course, public broadcasting can occasionally be controversial and provocative, as indeed it should be, and there are bound to be those who do not care for some of its programs, just as I do not care for everything funded by the National Endowments for the Arts and Humanities, which the Republican "culture" Pecksniffs also want to shut down. In a nation as large and diverse as ours, no single culture can dominate the country or be admired and accepted by everyone. I would not dream of demanding that my articulate, witty, and very conservative friend William F. Buckley, Jr., be taken off the air—even off public television—because I can always switch to another channel.

So can public broadcasting's detractors. Figuratively speaking, so can the two National Endowments' detractors. To permit the shutdown of these relatively small and low-cost sources of civilized enlightenment and enjoyment (especially when compared to the level of other governments' support of the arts) would mean surrender to the Philistines. I sympathize with those who say they are pained by the use of their tax funds to support words and works that they violently dislike, or who are pained by the use of their tax funds to support the federal financing of abortions, to which they are conscientiously opposed. I feel the same way about my tax dollars being used to support federal tobacco subsidies or the Central Intelligence Agency's employment of clairvoyants. But that's life in a free society.

I do not, however, object to Senator Dole's complaining to movie studios and record companies about excessive sex and violence in so many popular movies and song lyrics. Members of both parties have voiced such criticism. It is unfortunate that the senator appeared to exempt companies and performers known for their Republican leanings; it is even more unfortunate that he did not attack with equal vigor more elusive targets such as the right-wing voices of hate and violence on talk radio or in paranoid backwoods "militias," or even those whose products truly kill people, like gun manufacturers and tobacco companies. But Senator Dole's "culture" and mine differ, and such differences are hardly alarming in a free society.

More alarming are the Republicans who declared at their 1992 convention and subsequently that they have embarked upon a "cultural and religious war" in this country. "Cultural war" is a forgivable overstatement, like the "war on poverty," "war on crime," "war on drugs," "war on cancer," "war on AIDS," and other efforts that never lived up to that exaggerated description (and never succeeded). But the threat of a "religious war" in the United States is not to be taken lightly. Too much blood has been shed in recent years—in the Middle East, Northern Ireland, the Indian subcontinent, Central Asia, and even at the entrances to American abortion clinics—by fanatical fundamentalists invoking God's name and asserting that their victims were violating God's will.

The United States, founded and settled by people fleeing persecution and prizing religious liberty and tolerance, has generally been free of sectarian strife, particularly in the political arena. This has been due in large part to the Framers' insistence upon embodying in the Constitution and Bill of Rights and in such other notable documents as the Virginia Statute of Religious Freedom a high constitutional wall wholly separating church and state. Unlike foreign governments that either prefer or prosecute one or more religions, or governments that either stifle religion by dominating it or are themselves less free because some religious body dominates them, the United States neither establishes nor bans any particular denomination. Every citizen is free to attend or not attend, regularly or infrequently, the services of any one religious denomination, or many, or none at all.

No genuine place of worship or other religious institution is subject to tax here, and no taxpayer's funds are used to advance or retard any religious dogma or institution. No specific prayer or form of worship is either prescribed or proscribed, organized or opposed, by the state. All Americans are free to refrain from prayer or say their prayers if, as, when, and where they choose, in their own way and time, and in places public as well as private. Americans cannot be forced to become a captive audience to any particular gospel or financial supporters of the spreading of any creed. As Justice Hugo Black said long ago, no federal or state agency can by law or other action aid one religion, aid all religions, or prefer one religion over another.

This constitutional principle of keeping the government's hands off religion and vice versa has well served both church and state in this country for over two hundred years. When no one's religion is preferred by the state, everyone's religious liberty is safer. Behind this hospitable, not hostile, wall, the rights of all religious minorities (no single sect or denomination in this country has a majority) have been secure, and religion as a whole has flourished. These rights have been interpreted by a dozen major Supreme Court decisions, and were reinforced by the electorate's own deliberations and decision in the 1960 election.

Indeed, the United States today is one of the most religious nations in the world, with denominational membership and attendance at the highest levels. All genuine religious faiths are treated with respect, equality, and neutrality. Parents are free to send or not to send their children and their money to church-supported or other privately financed schools. No religious test can bar a prospect for either elected or appointed office. Clergymen, like the Reverend Pat Robertson and the Reverend Jesse Jackson, are free to run for any office, including the presidency; in 1960 a Catholic, John F. Kennedy, was elected President. He pledged to a convention of Protestant ministers in Houston that he believed in "an America that is officially neither Catholic,

Protestant, or Jewish . . . where no religious body seeks to impose its will directly or indirectly upon the general populace or on the public acts of its officials."

But this peaceful and precious separation of church and state is now under attack as never before by a religious group that does indeed seek to impose its will, both directly and indirectly, upon America's general populace and on the public acts of its officials. A well-organized, well-financed movement of white, evangelical born-again Christians and fundamentalists now seeks to take over the apparatus and ideology of the Republican Party, a party that once practiced a "big tent" approach and emphasized individual liberty, privacy, and privatization of the government's conduct of regulations, not government regulation of the private conduct of law-abiding citizens.

This movement is smoothly led by the Christian Coalition, founded by the Reverend Pat Robertson, a multimillionaire, multimedia mogul, preacher, and author. His 1991 book attributed Abraham Lincoln's assassination to "European bankers," a familiar euphemistic anti-Semitic slur. These religious-right activists, having proved in the 1994 elections that they could artfully manipulate religious tax exemptions and devout church members to elect both party and public officials, now dominate the Republican Party and its presidential nominating process in a substantial number of states.

They not only insist that the party endorse a constitutional amendment outlawing a woman's freedom of choice on abortion and select a presidential ticket that meets that particular litmus test, but insist as well on a variety of other breaches in the constitutional wall separating church and state, including Protestant prayer and other religious observances in the public schools and other taxpayer-supported institutions, broader taxpayer support for religious-school activities, an increased role for their tax-exempt church organizations in lobbying and politics, and the enforcement of chastity on the poor, homosexuals, and others.

One of their heroes, Republican columnist and television commentator Pat Buchanan, calls it "a holy war." One of their scourges, Republican Senator Arlen Specter of Pennsylvania, calls it "an effort through the Republican Party to write a new social order, starting with abortion and school prayer, saying 'Do it our way or else.'" Both of these gentlemen are right. For more than half a century, Americans have been doing battle against fanatical ideologues, around the world and at home, whether these zealots saluted the Nazi, Fascist, Communist, or other flag. We cannot stop now.

The Christian Coalition's leader, Ralph Reed, is fond of saying that its detractors are attacking religion and opposing people of faith. But this battle is not between religious believers and nonbelievers. In the United States, in the Middle East, and elsewhere, the battle is between fundamentalist zealots who wish to use their church to control the state, and the rest of us, of whatever faith, in all political parties, who understand, along with Mr. Justice Brandeis, that "the greatest dangers to liberty lurk in insidious encroachments by men of zeal, well-meaning but without understanding," and who sing, along with the psalmist, "how good and how pleasant it is for brethren to dwell together in unity."

One such missionary for ecumenical unity, now departed, was my father's youngest sister, a born-again Christian fundamentalist whose faith, as I remember it, had nothing in common with that of the Christian Coalition. She was devoted to serving the poor, not making scapegoats of them. She sought to help and forgive those whose views or vices she could not accept, not judge and turn them away. She preached love for people of all races, nations, and religions, not division and hate. And she accepted the Scriptural injunction "to do justice and to love kindness and to walk humbly with your God," in sharp contrast with today's religious-right preacher-politicians, whose legislative program features injustice and unkindness and who walk a walk that is anything but humble.

I never heard my aunt express concerns about the Supreme Court's constitutional ban on organized, mandated prayer in public schools. As President Kennedy noted soon after that decision, the best answer for parents who were concerned was to pray more at home with their children; their children were and remain free to pray on their own at school. Parents do not need any arm of the government to tell their sons and daughters where, when, how, or whether to pray.

Contrary to the dire pronouncements of the religious right, any public school child who wants to exercise his or her First Amendment right to say a prayer before a meal, an exam, or a football game is free to do so in his or her own way and words. Another child who wishes to pray in a different way or place, or to refrain from any prayer at all, also has a right under the First Amendment to do so. Neither of those children should be embarrassed or coerced by peer or teacher pressure into forgoing that individual right either by the prohibition of prayer or by the imposition of prescribed spoken prayers. Jewish, Moslem, Hindu, and other school children not of the Christian faith who somehow find themselves in private schools financed and operated by Christian Coalition adherents may have no choice but to be discomfited and disunited with their classmates in this fashion. But this should not be possible in the public schools of a united people.

Who could disagree with this arrangement, other than those

who wish to impose their own beliefs and ceremonies on all students and those who do not have the time or inclination to pray with their children at home? Unfortunately, unremitting but false warnings from the far right that the courts have shut all religion out of the public schools has caused some local school administrators to go far beyond constitutional requirements. Presumably to make sure their schools come within the law as they have wrongly heard it described, they have mistakenly banned noncompulsory prayers by individual students or groups, or teaching or talking about religion or the Bible (as distinguished from teaching or endorsing a particular religion), or the wearing of religious symbols and clothing in class. All such neutral and nonharassing religious activity and discussion are and long have been constitutionally permitted in public-school classrooms, as guidelines distributed last year by the U.S. Department of Education made clear.

Neither government nor public education in this country is "hostile" to religion, as some have alleged, nor should they be. Nevertheless, the leaders of the Republican religious right—who would in fact like to abolish the U.S. Department of Education—want far more than these activities already permitted. They want more even than organized prayers in the classroom. They want to amend the Constitution and Bill of Rights to provide public funding for religious schools and other institutions, to permit the mandating of Bible reading in the classroom as well as prayers, to allow state-supported expressions of religious preference in public-financed facilities and gatherings, and in effect to allow each community to decide whether its official prayers should be Christian, Jewish, or Moslem, and religious advice to be handed down from judge to jury, from guard to prisoner, from a military commander to his troops, and from government supervisors to their employees. A Constitution amended in that fashion would no longer guarantee equality before the law, which all religions now enjoy in the United States. It would, however, guarantee sectarian preferences, tensions, and power struggles in place of the peace and tranquillity that all religions teach.

None of these measures sought by the religious-right Republicans would advance the traditional works of the devout: to feed the hungry, to heal the sick, to shelter the homeless, to care for the child who has been forgotten. The Democratic Party's program is far more consistent with that universal religious tradition of caring, without all the moralizing, without the intrusive snooping into private conduct, and without the infringement of constitutionally protected rights of privacy and free choice in our personal lives and spirituality.

In urging on the 104th Congress a more compassionate approach to the poor, a Catholic bishop said, "It becomes easier for someone to understand God's presence when they have a sense of hope and renewal." Hope and renewal. I am usually skeptical about the value of political slogans. But if the Democratic Party is looking for a slogan for the twenty-first century, a brief reminder of the basic principles that continue to distinguish us from the Republicans, there it is in three simple words: hope and renewal. They sum up eloquently why I am a Democrat.

# ☆ CHAPTER 11 ☆
## MAINTAINING THE PEACE
☆ ☆ ☆

*I am an old-fashioned American patriot.* Having observed first hand several dozen countries in all parts of the world, and their legal, political, economic, and social systems, I enthusiastically endorse our own. Having experienced for nearly seven decades the remarkable freedoms, joys, and benefits of American life, as did my parents before me, I love this country as I could never love another. Though not blind to its faults, I do not hesitate when traveling abroad to defend the United States against the criticisms of foreign detractors, regardless of which party's policies or President is being deprecated.

This does not make me a closet "Republican" or distinguish me from other Democrats. Neither major party has a monopoly on patriotism. Each party pursues in foreign affairs the path that it believes best serves our national interests. Without minimizing the number and significance of their disagreements, one can say that the mainstreams of the two major parties currently flow together more than they diverge on major international matters—all campaign oratory to the contrary notwithstanding. Such disagreements as do exist are unlikely to be the basis for most citizens' choice between the Republicans and Democrats today. Only one such disagreement, discussed below, is so fundamental that it constitutes for me an important reason to be a Democrat.

Most Americans rarely choose between the parties on the basis of their respective foreign policy positions, even in years of international crisis. Certainly, today, in the absence of any serious foreign threat to our security, our citizens are preoccupied with their own economic problems and prospects and are understandably less concerned with the fate of people in far-off lands. They pay relatively less attention to world news and consider themselves poorly informed in that area.

Today's Congress and President are similarly focused on the domestic issues that are much more likely to determine election outcomes. After all, no single, sizable enemy commands our attention. Few if any of the current military battles around the world over ethnic, religious, boundary, and other local or internal conflicts seem likely to directly menace America's interests and safety. With the Cold War well behind us, with communism a shriveling ideology, with the arms race ended, apartheid vanquished in South Africa, the Israelis and Palestinians collaborating, and the shooting at least temporarily reduced in Central America, Angola, and Northern Ireland, most of the politically controversial hot spots in the world have cooled down. America's role as the only world superpower is unchallenged.

No doubt, foreign policy will still be an issue in the 1996 presidential campaign, particularly if any of the Clinton administration's successes in helping to bring relative stability to Russia, the Middle East, Haiti, North Korea, and the former Yugoslavia turn sour. At this writing, no one can foretell the outcome of the President's necessary and courageous leadership of NATO in enforcing a perilous peace in Bosnia. Both parties have been internally divided on the issue; Majority Leader Dole's statesmanlike support of the move could not convince a majority of his own party's members in Congress to support the President's deployment of forces to participate in the NATO effort. But, as stated at the outset, this book is intended to reflect my reasons for remaining a Democrat, not with respect only to this one year or one election or one President, but in general; not with respect to transitory issues that emerge and disappear from time to time, as many foreign policy issues do, but with respect to the broader, more basic principles on which the two parties clearly disagree.

When those disagreements involve such fundamental questions as economic fairness, religious liberty, racial justice, and governmental responsibility, bipartisan approaches are infrequent—what are parties for if not to be partisan? But a bipartisan approach to major foreign policy challenges that confront all of us together as Americans should be easier. As I wrote in my opening chapter, there is not, or at least need not be, an exclusively Republican or Democratic way of fighting international wars, terrorism, or drug traffic. Both parties want an America that is militarily and economically strong, that is the world's leader though not its policeman; a vigilant America, with reliable allies, that will promote peace and prevent war, promote democracy, and penalize dictatorship.

After World War Two, both parties cooperated with President Truman in launching NATO, the Marshall Plan, and the United Nations and Bretton Woods networks of international institutions, as well as the policy of Communist containment. In more recent years, similar bipartisan cooperation has backed the efforts made by Presidents of both parties on trade, nuclear nonproliferation, the Israeli-Palestinian peace process, and the isolation of terrorist states. Neither party wants an American military posture that is either gun-shy or trigger-happy.

Bipartisan agreement on broad objectives has never wholly eliminated either partisan debate or legislative executive squabbles on specific world problems, particularly when this country is at peace and particularly when the White House and Capitol Hill are controlled by different parties. The Constitution gives to the executive branch the initiative in foreign affairs but not a monopoly. Not surprisingly, both parties tend to act and speak in a more responsible, positive, and statesmanlike fashion on international matters when occupying the White House, and both tend to be more captious and less internationalist when in the opposition. In a complex and still dangerous world, leadership on foreign affairs for those primarily responsible is difficult, and criticism by those who are not primarily responsible is easy.

Democrats have justifiably argued that the current Republican Congress, in its partisan determination to oppose the current Democratic President, is trying to micromanage U.S. foreign policy, rock the boat globally, complicate and undermine the President's international initiatives, and unconstitutionally infringe upon exclusively presidential prerogatives. I would be more impressed by those arguments had I not earlier heard them voiced, almost word for word, by the Republicans back when the Democratic Congress was equally determined to oppose a Republican President.

Similarly, I would have been more impressed by Republican congressional complaints of ineptitude in this Democratic President's early handling of some foreign policy issues, including Bosnia, had I not recalled the bankruptcy of his two Republican predecessors' efforts in Lebanon, Iran, Central America, and numerous other places, including Bosnia. Both parties have found it difficult to shed many of the mind-sets of the Cold War, including the need for an enemy and for excessive arms and secrecy, and the division of the world into those who are with us and those who are against us. Both parties have found it difficult to shut down the outmoded military bases and wasteful weapons systems inherited from that era. Both parties, uncertain of China's future relations with the West after a change in leadership, have had difficulty pursuing a consistent approach to that nation. Both parties, largely for domestic political reasons, cling to old rigid policies on Cuba.

With the Cold War over, the dividing line between foreign and domestic policy and politics is more blurred than ever. On two aspects of foreign policy, the present general concurrence between the parties is at best tenuous and possibly temporary.

**Trade Policy**

Both parties endorse a policy of freer, not totally free, trade to expand America's export markets, as demonstrated in their stands on NAFTA, GATT, and the new World Trade Organization. If this country is to be a competitive leader in an increasingly globalized economy, that is the only rational choice for the nation as a whole. But for employees of older U.S. industries whose job and wage security is being devastated by foreign competition, the national economy's gain is their personal loss. Many of them cannot easily learn, much less move in order to take, new jobs requiring new skills in new locations. In addition, American workers blame (or are invited by free trade opponents to blame) foreign imports and the relocation of American plants abroad for the decline in real median wages, the worsening of income inequality, and the increasing job insecurity discussed earlier in these pages. If the choice is between protectionism and Republican-style "trickle down economics," with its faint hope that those profiting the most from increased trade and technology will spill some crumbs to those who do not, then more and more workers will prefer protectionism, and much of the Democratic Party's base of support for our trade policy will be ended.

The Democratic legislative agenda—neither trying to preserve the old economic order nor abandoning either those who still work in it or those in the higher-paying export industries who benefit from trade expansion—offers a more constructive choice. That is to invest in technology, research, and development to make certain that new industries are American-based, and to invest in people to make certain that those new industries can find the skills they need in this country. Investing in people means educating and retraining workers for new jobs in expanding industries, and encouraging labor-management cooperation, which enables all to share the gains of increased productivity. Meanwhile, help must be extended through the minimum wage and EITC to those left in low-paid work.

In addition, the Clinton administration has invoked on a global stage memories of Franklin Roosevelt's effort to get the economy going sixty years ago. Unemployment in the American national market, created in part by the movement of domestic companies and investors to low-wage states, was reduced by the New Deal's imposition of nationwide fair labor standards: a minimum wage, a maximum work week, and the abolition of child labor and sweatshops. In today's world, where industry and investors in an integrated global market can take advantage in developing countries of unduly low wages, ineffective environmental protection, and the use of child labor, prison labor, or even slave labor in some of them, a new effort is necessary. The aim should be to gradually elevate wage and other standards to an acceptable sliding-scale minimum consistent with each nation's rate of economic growth and productivity. This will be no easy task, and must become not a unilateral protectionist tool but a universal tool to improve the lot of all. Republicans, who must worry about a revival in their ranks of their own traditional protectionism, have never taken kindly to any labor or environmental standards or to the agenda of investment in research and people described above. Democrats do, and the enactment of their program is essential to stave off protectionism.

## Moral Foundations of U.S. Foreign Policy

Both parties pay lip service to the moral foundations of foreign policy in this country. More than any other great power in history, the United States has in the years since World War Two—with some notable exceptions—demonstrated forgiveness and generosity for the civilian populations of its former enemies, humanitarianism for foreign countries wracked by war, poverty, or natural disaster, and fidelity regarding its allies and international obligations. Over the years we have taken the lead in urging and aiding international cooperation, economic development, human rights, democratization, and an end to colonial rule. Since the days of Woodrow Wilson, Franklin Roosevelt, and Harry Truman, Democrats have generally been in the forefront of those endeavors—though not always without dissent and division. Many Republicans, in contrast, prefer to ignore moral considerations in foreign policy as "soft-headed" or "sentimental" and favor a narrower, more calculated balance-of-power expediency.

Neither approach can be used exclusively, but history tells us that U.S. foreign policy ventures that ignore our traditional public values cannot be long sustained.

Morality versus expediency in foreign affairs has also constituted a philosophical fault line within the Democratic Party, one that cracked wide open in 1968 as a result of the war in Vietnam. That internal party dispute, like the simultaneous battle within the party over civil rights, divided and depleted the Democratic Party. Out of increasing revulsion to the military draft, the casualties, and the war's expansion by the Nixon administration, a wave of timid "blame America" neo-isolationism swept through much of our party, sweeping aside the history of its greatest twentieth-century leaders and their willingness to stand up for American principles and interests abroad. Other Democrats argued with equal passion that our Cold War leadership and commitments required America to stay the course in Vietnam. In between were those who acknowledged America's obligations to intervene internationally when necessary but argued that after the futile expenditure of so many lives and years in Vietnam, our continued entanglement on behalf of the undemocratic, uncooperative, and ineffective South Vietnamese government was neither wise nor necessary.

When those passions finally subsided, a rough new national—not merely Democratic but national—sense had emerged broadly defining both the role and the limits of American military intervention abroad. Today, both parties and the American people as a whole recognize in very general terms our obligations as the principal defender of freedom in the world, including our obligation to use force when necessary. But both parties prefer a high threshold for any massive deployment of American armed forces into potential combat situations unless our vital national interests are directly engaged; our military mission is clearly defined, limited, and achievable; our prospects for early success and exit are promising; and long-term allied, congressional, and public support appear certain.

The enduring solidity of even this broad and imprecise consensus in the nation and within each of the major parties may be unknown until severely tested by some more risky and ambiguous military challenge in a more crucial area than those posed in recent years on the world's periphery. For the present, however, the old-fashioned Fortress America, keep-our-boys-home no-matter-what, "no entangling alliances" isolationism is not a dominant force in either party, despite bipartisan concerns about American forces in Bosnia and despite Pat Buchanan's vigorous quadrennial efforts to push the Republicans in that direction.

Unfortunately, two new forms of isolationism have become dominant in the ranks of congressional Republicans, and these do constitute that one foreign policy difference between the parties today that is reason enough for me, and no doubt many others, to choose the Democrats. The first might be termed "fiscal isolationism": not an unwillingness to lead the world but an unwillingness to pay the financial cost of that leadership. The second could be termed "unilateralist isolationism": not an unwillingness to act in international affairs but an unwillingness to do so in genuine collaboration with others.

Fiscal isolationism, or "back-door isolationism," as Clinton's national security adviser, Anthony Lake, termed it, is the posture of those who "champion American leadership but . . . want it the one way you can't have it, and that's on the cheap." This country's world leadership, which serves both our national security and our economic interests in myriad ways, relies today less on the actual use of American arms than on American diplomacy, food, technical and development assistance, ideas, and outreach. Like our defense establishment, where spending on readiness is now at an all-time high level, the readiness levels of our diplomatic establishment depend upon sufficient quantities of highly trained and strategically deployed personnel, adequate facilities, and modern equipment. Unfortunately, the Republicans are withholding the funding necessary for that readiness.

Speaker Gingrich acknowledged last year that the Defense Department budget substantially exceeded the amount actually needed to defend the United States because this excess represented the premium our country must pay to fulfill its role as world leader. His point is well taken. Congress overfunded the military budget last year by some $20 billion to $40 billion or more in order to fulfill that leadership role, to the point where we are spending nearly as much on defense as the rest of the world combined. At the same time we are underfunding an already depleted but equally essential diplomatic budget by $1.2 billion. That amount is peanuts to the Pentagon but vital to the diplomats; it represented the largest single such reduction in the diplomatic budget in American history and made no sense at all— unless we were planning to lead the world solely by sending our armed forces into harm's way. As Secretary of State Warren Christopher has said, "Diplomacy and force . . . are indivisible instruments of American power."

Why require some fifty American embassies and consulates to lower the American flag and close up shop? A small neutral country need not have diplomatic posts in virtually every world capital, but the world's leader should. Our diplomatic outposts, libraries, and information centers are literally our first line of defense and our best source of foreign intelligence; Deputy Secretary of State Strobe Talbott observed that cuts like those "turn the American eagle into an ostrich."

Why cut the funds promised to help Russia finance the dismantlement of its nuclear weapons, a goal we spent four decades and trillions of dollars to achieve? Destroying strategic weapons on the ground now is much cheaper and more reliable than later trying to intercept and destroy them in the air when they are en route to the United States.

Why cut the already small amount of humanitarian and development assistance provided to those free but struggling nations whose support we wooed during the Cold War, whose friendship (and U.N. votes) we will need again, whose markets and natural resources are essential to our own economy, and whose desperate future without our help would be wholly inconsistent with the stable, peaceful world we seek? President Eisenhower called foreign economic assistance America's "best investment," but, even before these latest cuts, we were last among the twenty-one industrialized nations of the world in the percentage of GNP devoted to such assistance.

Why cut the few millions of dollars in U.S. seed money needed, along with billions of dollars from South Korea and Japan, to implement the agreement freezing North Korea's nuclear development and consequently saving us hundreds of millions of dollars or more in military force expansion in Northeast Asia?

This miserly approach to the essential cost of world diplomatic leadership is not merely a policy of congressional budget cutting—it is a policy of cut and run. To assert that this retreat from the world is fiscally required is ludicrous. The entire International Affairs Budget of the United States Government represents less than 1.5 percent of the total federal budget. For the most wealthy and least taxed nation in the industrialized world to reduce further its already shrunken foreign policy budget can only undermine American diplomacy and leadership for years to come, regardless of which party occupies the White House. These measures do not save scarce resources but squander precious assets. Some Republicans called these 1995 cuts responsible frugality, "putting America first." In reality, it was irresponsible demagoguery, hurting America most.

"Unilateralist isolationism" makes even less sense. Republican campaign speakers have repeatedly stressed two points: first, that the post–Cold War world is a disorganized and dangerous place, and that America's strategic and economic interests depend upon the rule of law and order and thus on curbing any threatening outbreaks of instability and violence; second, that America's leadership role does not include taking on the role of Lone Ranger and world policeman and risking only America's blood and fortune in far-flung fields of battle. Right on both counts. But why, then, do the Republicans insist on blocking our full participation in the multilateral regional and global organizations that we helped establish to share the tasks and risks of resolving and containing those local conflagrations before they spread?

Surely we know by now that we cannot single-handedly halt the movement across boundaries and oceans of war, terrorism, weapons, AIDS, drugs, illegal immigrants, pestilence, or pollution. It would be an incomprehensible strategy to undertake to fight a nation that is sufficiently dangerous to worldwide peace and security to constitute a threat to our own vital interests, or to arm that nation's foes or blockade its borders or even negotiate with its leaders, without seeking the participation, assistance, or advice of our friends and allies. We would not receive even a passing grade in an elementary course on statecraft if we assumed or accepted that allied participation without due regard and respect for their particular concerns and contributions. To be a leader requires followers. To be team captain requires consideration of the views and needs of other players. "Going it alone" may sound great in Fourth of July rhetoric, but "facing the world alone" does not.

It is true that consultation with other governments can be a nuisance when decisive, quick international action is required. Coordination can be logistically difficult. Consideration of other nations' interests can be stifling. Cooperation can undermine this and every other nation's ultimate obligation to do whatever best serves its own cause.

But in order to lead, we must keep our friendships and our word. It was irresponsible in the extreme for the Republican Congress to blithely reverse the solemn commitments constitutionally made by the Presidents of both parties to our collaborators on the world stage. Last year, for example, the Republican Congress refused to honor President Bush's earlier commitment of U.S. matching funds to the World Bank's low-interest loan window, known as the International Development Association; these funds were designed to help reform economies and open markets in the world's poorest countries with feasible, profitable projects that private investors would nevertheless never initiate. That kind of irresponsible vote is not macho but myopic, risking over the long run not only our leadership but our interests as well.

The fiscal and unilateral isolationists also joined hands in slashing our pledged contributions to the Inter-American Development Bank and other regional development banks; to the International Atomic Energy Agency (despite the agency's role in ferreting out Iraq's secret nuclear preparations); to the World Health Organization, now battling AIDS as it once successfully battled smallpox and polio; even to NATO itself, in the midst of its first combat and peace enforcement operations in history.

Not all of these heedless violations of our international obligations bore the fig-leaf of fiscal responsibility. The former Reagan defense official Lawrence Korb called Reagan's multi-billion-dollar Strategic Defense Initiative the "litmus test of loyalty to the Reagan legacy, the foreign policy equivalent of abortion." Once known as Star Wars, now reborn and rechristened the National Missile Defense System, it still carries a staggering price tag. Its sponsors call for the early development and nationwide deployment of a land-based system to intercept long-range ballistic missiles. Inasmuch as the demise of the Russian military leaves not even one potential enemy in a position during this decade to launch a strategic missile against the United States mainland, it is unclear whose missiles these hundreds of billions of dollars would be spent to intercept.

But crystal clear to all is the fact that such a deployment would constitute an outright violation of the 1972 Anti–Ballistic Missile (A.B.M.) Treaty on which our subsequent pyramid of nuclear arms control agreements was based. Those agreements, including START I and START II and even the 1968 Nuclear Nonproliferation Treaty would all unravel, along with our security, once Russia and other nations found the United States upsetting a basic premise of those agreements by aggressively withdrawing from ABM. START I and II, when implemented, will destroy a lot more nuclear warheads than this new system ever could, even if it worked. Even former Joint Chiefs chairman and Reagan SDI supporter Colin Powell has deplored this repudiation of the ABM Treaty.

Other treaties, equally meritorious, all carefully negotiated, mutually beneficial, and fully verifiable and enforceable, all signed by most nations of the world, were blocked last year in the Republican Senate:

- The treaty banning the manufacture and use of poison gas and other chemical weapons, termed by *The Washington Post* the "most powerful and comprehensive arms control agreement ever negotiated," can only help this country halt the development by Russia and others of weapons we have already renounced and are anxious to see banished. But if this treaty goes into effect without us, the United States will have no voice in its implementation and no standing to persuade Russia to ratify. To the best of my knowledge, the only world leaders who oppose the treaty are Saddam Hussein, Muammar al-Qaddafi, and Republican Senator Jesse Helms.
- The revised Law of the Sea Treaty, still not ratified even after its alteration to meet our objections regarding deep-sea mining, is essential to the U.S. Navy's ability to project our military presence quickly when distant conflicts threaten.
- The International Biodiversity Convention to save the world's flora and fauna has been ratified by virtually every country in the world, including all of the major industrialized nations—except for us, the world's "leader."

But all of these unilateralist isolationist positions adopted by the Republican Party last year pale by comparison with its assault on the United Nations. Despite its bureaucratic excesses and disorganization, the United Nations has over the last fifty-one years delivered food, medicine, humanitarian and technical assistance, development funds, democratization expertise, literacy aids, environmental improvements, election monitors, refugee relief, family planning kits, and innumerable other services to millions of people and thousands of communities around the globe, services without which the world would be a wretched place and the United States a poorer nation.

The United Nations also provides a global marketplace for diplomatic ideas, the major meeting ground for the developed and undeveloped worlds, the globe's most useful source of international law and human rights standards, and coordination for the widest possible range of assistance to the widest possible range of countries. The attention of the American media, unfortunately, has been focused in recent years almost exclusively on the United Nation's most difficult role, international peacekeeping—especially difficult when it lacks the full and adequate support of the United States government.

In a world without U.N. peacekeepers, U.S. forces would have been left alone in Korea, the Persian Gulf, and Haiti. Without U.N. peacekeepers, conflicts that were merely expanded or prolonged by U.S. involvement—in Cambodia, Nicaragua, El Salvador, and Angola—might well have continued indefinitely. Without U.N. peacekeepers, usually aided by United States logistical and other support, conflicts in the Middle East, Cyprus, Mozambique, Namibia, Indonesia, and elsewhere might have continued indefinitely. Without U.N. peacekeepers, even in the much criticized operations in Bosnia, Croatia, Somalia, and Rwanda, millions more innocent civilians would have lost their lives to savagery or starvation.

And yet the Republicans set out last year on a path toward a world without U.N. peacekeepers. They sought to eliminate our 1995–96 funding obligation for peacekeeping, to sharply cut and condition future funding for U.S. participation, to prohibit the Department of Defense from providing logistical help for emergency U.N. peacekeeping—essentially to terminate our forty years of support for this essential U.N. function. Such a violation of our treaty obligations invites other countries to do the same. In time the results will be the withdrawal of U.N. forces from Iraq's borders, the Israeli-Syrian border, and more than a dozen other trouble spots around the globe, including Cambodia, Kashmir, and Haiti.

An oft-repeated Republican fear motivating this withdrawal is the danger that U.S. participation in U.N. peacekeeping might lead to U.S. personnel serving under a foreign commander. In our history, hundreds of thousands, if not millions, of U.S. troops have served under foreign commanders—starting with the American Revolution and Lafayette—just as foreign troops have served under U.S. commanders. How else can an allied coalition deploy its forces flexibly?

To put this fear in perspective: a little over 1.57 million men and women wear the U.S. military uniform today. Of those, a little over 1.57 million are *not* involved in U.N. peacekeeping. As of this writing, fewer than 1,000 Americans are among the 62,000 troops participating in seventeen United Nations operations around the world (not including NATO forces in Bosnia). At last count, nineteen other countries were each contributing more forces to U.N. peacekeeping than the United States—tiny Jordan is contributing more than three times as many as we are—and nineteen countries have also sustained more peacekeeping fatalities than the United States. Yet scores of American politicians, some of whom unaccountably continued to support the U.S. war in Vietnam after 50,000 U.S. fatalities, turned against the United Nations after the tragic deaths in Somalia of eighteen U.S. servicemen under U.S. command on a U.S.–inspired mission.

I have had some involvement with the United Nations, and my wife considerably more. I fully acknowledge that its flaws and failings are manifest and manifold. It is neither more wise nor more far-sighted than the governments that compose it, and is subject to the same kind of waste, inefficiency, and abuse. It will never become a world government, or command its own army, or be able to alter its ways or those of its 185 members quickly— and that is just as well. Republicans in Congress complain that U.N. actions are micromanaged by its members, and no one can doubt their expertise on the subject of micromanagement. But imposing our will unilaterally in blunderbuss fashion and eviscerating U.N. peacekeeping are not the ways to reform an organization badly in need of reform.

Particularly ironic was the Congress's insistence on further financial reforms in an organization whose regular budget, unlike our own, has had zero real growth for many years, and for which Congress has consistently failed for many years to appropriate the funds owed by the United States for its membership dues and peacekeeping assessments. Unlike Britain, Canada, Australia, and other members paid up in full, the United States, beginning in the Reagan administration, surpassed even Russia and Ukraine in our delinquency. "U.N. bashing is especially irritating," said Canada's Prime Minister, "when it comes from those not paying their bills." "Representation without taxation," chided the British. "The world's biggest deadbeat," chanted a chorus of other leaders. But the U.S. Senate, oblivious to shame, upon hearing that a few United Nations ambassadors were behind in their rent and other financial obligations to New York landlords and merchants, proceeded to threaten, in a new resolution introduced by Senator Jesse Helms, to cut U.S. payments to the United Nations by another $10 million unless the U.N. Secretary General helped crack down on "deadbeat diplomats."

Ludicrous, but sad. It is even sadder that Republican leaders have made the United Nations a domestic political football in the current political campaign. This could be expected of militia fanatics who say they are arming against a U.N. takeover. But more might have been expected of Senate Majority Leader Dole, who launched his presidential candidacy with a speech in which he deliberately mispronounced the name of United Nations Secretary-General Boutros Boutros-Ghali, vowed to "stop placing the agenda of the United Nations before the interests of the United States," and pledged that "American policies will be determined by us, not by the United Nations."

What an applause line! What invigorating pugnacity! What nonsense. No American policies have ever been determined by the United Nations. No U.N. initiative ever could have survived a U.S. veto, had that initiative been deemed inimical to our interests. No American political leader favors surrendering that right of veto. Nor does any Democrat want "to subordinate the United States to the United Nations," which Speaker Gingrich calls President Clinton's "multinational fantasy." How sad that U.N. peacekeeping, once a centerpiece of President Bush's New World Order, became a central target for virtually all the 1995–96 Republican presidential candidates, with the notable and admirable exception of Senator Richard Lugar.

Under this kind of fire, the Clinton administration's support of the United Nations has often been weak and inconsistent. But if both parties would participate more actively and positively, this country could help reform, reorganize, and revitalize the United

Nations. We can participate in reexamining and restraining its reliance on peacekeeping operations, particularly in hostile situations where there is no peace to be kept. Without greater U.S. engagement and support, this will not happen, and the United States will gradually lose a valuable instrument "to save succeeding generations from the scourge of war," the goal so eloquently set forth in the U.N. charter.

If this country continues to pursue the Republican path of fiscal and unilateralist isolationism, and to renege on our obligations to the United Nations, NATO, and other allies and international organizations, we will fatally compromise our role as world leader, erode our credibility, and encourage all the rogues and despots now in power who prefer a lawless world. No Republican and no Democrat wants that kind of world. For the most part, the parties are in commendable concurrence as to what they support in foreign affairs. But, in one area, they differ sharply as to what they oppose. The Republican Party of today, unlike its predecessors, opposes sensible United States participation in multilateralism. The Democratic Party does not. That makes me pleased that I am a Democrat.

# ☆ CHAPTER 12 ☆
## PREPARING FOR VICTORY
☆ ☆ ☆

*I like to be on the winning side.* As a Cornhusker football fan, I know the satisfaction of repeated victory. As a New York Mets baseball fan, I know the pain of defeat. Having been involved in countless dozens of political campaigns since my youth, I have experienced both winning and losing—and winning is a lot more fun.

Why, then, do I continue to identify with a political party that some say will never win again? I was cautioned separately by two sensible, well-meaning friends, when I told them my plans to write this book, that I was "too late" and "swimming against the tide." They did not urge me to become a Republican; they simply urged that I accept the *New York Times* prediction last year that the nation was witnessing "the end of the Democratic Party as Americans know it today—if not now, within a matter of years."

I disagree. I believe that the Democratic Party, more moderate than the new Republican extremists, more concerned with the economic security issues that underlie the electorate's anxiety, and less divided on matters of race, peace, and philosophy than at any time in modern Democratic Party history, has every opportunity to become the majority party once again—if it will make the most of that opportunity.

Certainly the hard numbers most often emphasized by the news media in 1995 appeared to support their dire predictions of Democratic doom. In 1994, the Democrats lost heavily, disastrously, across the board—the majority of congressional, senatorial, gubernatorial, and state legislative election contests and consequently their majorities among governors and state legislatures as well as in the U.S. Senate and House. Republican candidates for the U.S. House of Representatives outpolled their Democratic opponents in virtually every region, particularly the South, increasing their percentage of votes cast for Republican House candidates to a level almost one third higher than it had been in the last midterm congressional election in 1990, the largest such gain in history. Not a single incumbent Republican senator, governor, or member of congress lost a race for reelection.

Particularly discouraging was the extent to which Democratic candidates were rejected by voters who were Democrats, or had once been Democrats, or should be Democrats. Some of them voted Republican and more of them simply stayed home. Voter participation usually declines in midterm elections, but in 1994, people whose votes were instrumental in the Democratic victory of 1992—first-time voters, young voters, "down scale" voters at the lower end of the income and education scales, black and Hispanic voters—stayed home in extra large numbers, while turnout increased in the voter categories more likely to vote Republican.

On paper, the Democratic Party's statistical outlook for 1996 and beyond is bleak. No Democrat has been elected twice to the White House since Franklin Roosevelt. The few states in which the Democrats attracted more voters than the Republicans in 1994 have a total of 73 electoral votes compared to the Republicans' 450. In the last seven presidential elections, Democrats have lost five of those elections, getting in all seven an average of only 43 percent of the vote. Virtually all political analysts last year predicted further congressional losses for the Democrats in 1996, particularly in the Senate, which would bring their total in that chamber to its lowest level in almost three generations.

Pundits saw in 1994 a long-term trend. Southern voters, male voters, and Catholic and other churchgoing voters had been drifting away from the Democratic Party for some years. Many of the Democratic House seats lost in 1994 were seats that the party had barely or rarely won in recent times. Nineteen ninety-four's declining turnout in Democratic-leaning voter categories was not new, and may well worsen. In contrast, nearly all Protestant married male college graduates between the ages of thirty and seventy who are currently employed full-time and are earning more than $50,000 a year turned out to vote in 1994—and most of them voted Republican.

Many of the key components of F.D.R.'s winning Democratic coalition sixty years ago are fragmented or in disarray. The defection of the South, which began in the 1960s as a result of the Democratic Party's leadership on civil rights, now appears complete. The Northern big cities have lost a substantial portion of their white voters to the Republican suburbs and Sun Belt states. Labor union families have sharply declined both as a percentage of the workforce and in their Democratic Party loyalties. Farmers are fewer in number and mostly Republican. Voter turnout remains low among blacks, Hispanics, the young, the poor, and the unskilled; and many younger voters and many Hispanic voters, especially older Cuban Americans, are fiercely Republican. Nine of the ten largest states are today under the control of Republican governors who have little interest in urban problems. Roosevelt in his day might well have held a Democratic Party strategy session with the governors of Michigan and Mississippi, the mayors of New York and Los Angeles, a Farm Belt populist, and a building-trades union leader. Today they would all be Republicans.

Constantly predicting defeat can become a self-fulfilling prophecy, especially for legislators who see little prospect of regaining the power and perquisites that come with membership in the majority, or who are pessimistic about surviving the next round of redistricting in states now controlled by the other party. Thus, it is not surprising that in 1995 and 1996 a disturbingly large number of elected Democratic officeholders, particularly in Texas and the South, announced either their retirement or their switch of allegiance to the Republican camp—more switches than at any other time in this century. The defections and departures led the columnist Maureen Dowd to speak of "the incredible shrinking party." Large numbers of very conservative Southern Democratic congressmen have become very conservative Southern Republican congressmen. Other Democratic officeholders publicly backed away not from the party name but from its record and philosophy.

Not surprisingly, many political analysts concluded that the massive Republican victory of 1994 was a "party realignment" election like that of 1932, confirmatory evidence that party loyalties had permanently switched and that the electoral tide had definitively turned for the next generation or longer. Such a realignment would consign the Democratic Party either to disintegration and extinction like the mid-nineteenth-century Whigs, or to the long-term minority impotence that largely characterized the Democrats for most of the period between 1896 and 1932 and the Republicans between 1932 and 1968. Throughout most of 1995, the Democratic Party, hemorrhaging both leaders and followers, was understandably termed "a party under siege," lacking both credibility and prospects.

Not so fast. Under siege, yes. But not vanquished. First, losing an election—even losing several elections—is no cause to disband a party, or even to despair. Losing the public allegiance of elected officials who had long ago rejected the party's basic principles is no great loss. Candidates and parties who learn from their losses fare better over the long run than those for whom winning is everything, the only "principle," candidates who will do anything to win at any price, whatever the cost to our sense of national community and to their own reputation for integrity.

The Republicans did not quit the field after Landon's overwhelming defeat by Roosevelt in 1936 or Goldwater's overwhelming defeat by Johnson in 1964, despite the fact that they occurred during a period of thirty-six long years (1933–69) with only one Republican President. The Democratic Party did not disband when it endured the previous thirty-six years (1897–1933) with only one Democratic President. Like a Holmes or Brandeis dissent, ideas proposed in losing campaigns or by losing parties and their representatives in Congress, or even by third parties with no representation in Congress, have often become the accepted wisdom in later years. Nebraska's George Norris, whose lonely fights on principle echoed in victories decades later and whose landmark legislative proposals reverberated years after he first introduced them, truly believed that "whatever use I have been to progressive civilization has been accomplished in the things I [initially] failed to do."

More important, less than 37 percent of the eligible population actually voted in 1994, and the Republicans won little more than one half of that vote; I do not believe that a Republican victory based on 19 percent of the American electorate—only their third victory in the House of Representatives in sixty-four years—constitutes proof of a permanent Republican realignment. The overall vote for the Republicans in 1994's Senate, House, and gubernatorial contests was under 54 percent—not an irreversible margin: consider President Bush's 90 percent job approval rating in 1991, one year before he lost.

The two parties are still roughly equal in terms of party identification, but, more important, that identification means less in terms of commitment and loyalty today than it has at any time in modern history. The pattern of public volatility—independent registration and voting and party switching—is so high that neither party has a majority lock on either the electorate or the electoral college. If President Clinton is reelected in 1996, each party will have won exactly half of the last ten presidential elections. Our nation is in all likelihood headed for a prolonged period of frequently shifting party prospects and majorities—not realignment so much as "dealignment," one scholar has noted, a turning away from both major parties and from politics in general.

The Democrats are not entering this uncertain period totally devoid of assets. It is true that they lost badly among Southerners, white males, and the well-to-do in 1994. They fared better among female voters, particularly younger women; they fared better in many of the Northern and Eastern states and some of the Western and Midwestern states, and they were strongly preferred by voters committed to civil rights and to environmental preservation. Most important, if all registered Democrats had turned out to vote in 1994 and had voted Democratic, our party would have won by a landslide. The slight increase in midterm election turnout that year was due mostly to Republican voters. Over 60 percent of American families with annual incomes exceeding $50,000 voted, compared with only 27 percent of those with incomes below $15,000. Next time, with more targeted registration and get-out-the-vote efforts, the result could be different.

It is true that for the long run the Democrats appear to face a shortage of moderate and nationally known leaders—but so do the Republicans. The Republican leaders who are moderate are not nationally known, and those who are nationally known are not moderate.

It is true that once-Democratic voters have left the big cities for the suburbs and the Sun Belt, where many of them convert to Republicanism. But many moderate and pragmatic newcomers to those areas are unhappy with the extremism of the Republican program, particularly the intrusiveness of the far right and the threat to religious liberty posed by the Christian Coalition. If religious zealots succeed in dominating the Republican Party's platform and in nominating the Republican Party's ticket, I believe most of suburbia will vote Democratic. Moreover, population increases in the Sun Belt and suburbs resulting from that very migration are creating environmental and educational problems that Democrats are deemed by the public to be better able to solve.

It is true that not one of the three Democratic Presidents between Roosevelt and Clinton who contemplated a second elected term (Truman in 1952, Johnson in 1968, and Carter in 1980,

Kennedy having been assassinated in midterm) was returned to the White House. But each of them was strongly opposed for the Democratic Party's nomination, which weakened his prospects for victory in the general election—an experience that a more united Democratic Party will not face in 1996 and need not repeat in the future.

It is true that the differences between the two parties on affirmative action and civil rights have driven many Southern whites out of the Democratic Party. But millions of Southern whites in the past voted for Truman, Kennedy, Johnson, Carter, and Clinton, despite disagreeing with those Presidents on race, because they recognized that the Democratic Party was on their side on economic issues. Today's Southern white voters, like their counterparts in the rest of the country, are far more educated and sophisticated, and consequently more tolerant and less prejudiced. Furthermore, Republican pandering to racists offends many voters in all regions. Republican Jack Kemp has already said, "I don't want to be in a party that's all white," and that sense of discomfort may well cause many undecided Southern whites to vote Democratic again.

Finally, it is true that the Republican Party won the House of Representatives in 1994 with its largest share of that vote since 1946. But the 1946 victory by the Republican 80th Congress was overturned only two years later, when the Democrats regained control of both houses of Congress and sent Harry Truman back to the White House.

Of course the candidates and issues were different, and it was an era when party affiliation and appeal had a much stronger effect. Nevertheless, it is clear that taking the reins of legislative responsibility during a difficult and uncertain postwar transitional period (whether that war was "hot" or "cold") is a mixed political blessing for the lucky party.

Congress's harshest cuts in middle-class programs have been mostly phased to kick in only toward the end of the new seven-year budget cycle. But, long before then, the voters, especially the Independents, the Perot supporters, the swing voters, the disgruntled Democrats and moderate Republicans, may well see and feel and, I believe, reject the cynicism and approach of the Republican "revolution." After all, it is the only "revolution" in this country's history to redistribute wealth and government benefits from the middle class, the weak, and the vulnerable upward to the affluent and powerful.

Eventually, American workers will see that their grim job, health-care, and retirement insecurities, aggravated by the spiraling income gap and the downward drag on wages, continue unabated. They will see that little or no progress has been made by the new congressional majority in reducing crime on the streets or special-interest power in Washington, much less in fulfilling campaign promises. They will see that higher Medicare premiums, fewer student loans, and a dirtier environment are a high price to pay for Republican tax cuts that worsen the deficit but bring very little benefit to most taxpayers. Republican House Budget Committee Chairman John Kasich prophesied, I think correctly, "If this process . . . turns into just cutting spending on people who don't have lobbyists, we lose."

That was indeed the process, and the people who do have lobbyists—the defense contractors, the antienvironmental companies, the religious right, the special business interests—do not constitute a winning coalition.

In short, it will be the Republicans' turn to tell the voters that deficits and taxes cannot both be cut without cutting favorite programs, and that controversial legislation cannot be enacted without making compromises. It will be the Republicans' turn to try holding together the disparate wings of *their* party, all of them angered over the party's failure to deliver on most of its promises: its moderates and entrepreneurs combating the hard right; the new federalist deficit hawks combating the supply-side tax cutters; and the libertarians and women's rights advocates combating the Christian Coalition.

Republican presidential primaries drive their presidential hopefuls still further to the right. In the years 1996, 2000, and beyond, their nominees will have a more difficult time scrambling back to the center in full view of the press and public. My conviction is that most voters, whatever their religious beliefs or gender, will instinctively back away from the harshness in social matters, the meddling in private matters, and the extremism in economic matters that today's Republican leaders have demonstrated.

But, say the more cynical experts, all these arguments count for little in an election campaign compared to one major factor: money. Democratic senators and representatives, no longer controlling Congress, congressional committees, and the action agenda of each, will no longer be able to match, much less surpass, the Republicans in successfully soliciting contributions from the wealthy individuals and big-business PACs that have never been enthusiastic about the Democratic philosophy.

The crucial and increasing importance of money to the outcome of any political contest cannot be denied. Any candidate who substantially outspends his opponent wins roughly 90 percent of the time. In 1984, a Twentieth Century Fund task force condemned the "uncontrolled, upward spiral in campaign contributions and expenditures" that forced "candidates to raise ever-increasing sums of money" and called for prompt remedial action. But ten years later congressional candidates spent nearly twice as much, $724 million; PAC spending exceeded $180 million; a House candidate had to raise an average of $516,000 to be elected; a Senate candidate, $4.4 million. Even this was dwarfed by 1992, the latest presidential campaign year, when all campaigns for all offices cost $3.2 billion, of which more than half a billion dollars was spent in the presidential race alone.

What a tragedy that the world's leading democracy features the world's most expensive political campaign system, requiring most candidates in both parties to spend a majority of their campaign hours not discussing or studying issues, but participating in a process that inherently smacks of conflicts of interest and corruption in at least four different ways:

1. *Quid Pro Quo?* The incumbent or future legislator needs what the potential donor has: money with which to purchase the commercials and television time, the consulting and polling services, and the other media and staff support needed for the campaign. The potential donor needs what the incumbent or future legislator has or will have: a voice and a vote in favor of a particular tax cut, regulation reduction, pork-barrel project or other public measure favoring that donor's private interests, or a voice and a vote against a particular public measure that would protect workers, consumers, or the environment by limiting, in the public interest,

that donor's commercial activities. They need each other and they will for years to come, and they both know it.

2. *Inequal Treatment?* Hard-working legislators and their staffs, whose schedules are almost always overcrowded trying to fulfill committee, subcommittee, political, and other obligations, necessarily have only a limited amount of time to meet with constituents, both in Washington and back home. Is a noncontributor with a worthy cause likely to receive the same time and attention that is granted by these public servants to a large contributor seeking the legislator's intervention with a regulatory agency or a congressional committee? Is a candidate or incumbent likely to ask Congress to regulate, investigate, or tax the pollution, price increases, profiteering, or other unworthy practices of any individual, industry, or company whose name is high on his list of major campaign contributors?

3. *Unequal Influence?* Large and successful business executives, their corporations, and their well-financed trade organizations and lobbyists in Washington can all afford to make political campaign contributions of a size that the recipient won't forget. Those at the other end of the income scale cannot.

4. *Unfair Advantage?* Candidates who are personally wealthy, under a Supreme Court decision constitutionally protecting campaign expenditures as free speech, can finance an elaborate campaign without

spending the time and energy involved in soliciting funds in small amounts from hundreds and thousands of others. A candidate of modest means, no matter how meritorious, cannot.

I trust that no member of Congress or other officeholder in this country is explicitly for sale. Stated exchanges of votes for money, I trust, no longer occur. But none are necessary to give monied interests an unfair advantage over the public interest, to give sizable contributors an unfair advantage over small or non-contributors, to give millionaires, who now populate much of the Senate, an unfair advantage over other candidates, and to keep out of the winner's column—and often out of the race altogether—a superior and dedicated individual who cannot compete financially. The influence of big money on the few highly publicized, highly controversial issues on which each party is united or public opinion makes itself strongly heard is likely to be minimal. But the influence of big money on some little-noticed tax loophole or some regulatory exemption or some quiet corporate subsidy is maximum.

Politicians in both parties know this is true—and they know it is wrong. Many of them regard fundraising as an unseemly, distasteful necessity, and they know that their pandering to the wishes of special-interest contributors is worse. But over the years too many incumbents in both parties could not bring themselves to renounce, either unilaterally or through genuine reform legislation, the advantages that their official positions gave them in both raising and spending money. One result is that the rate of reelection to the House among incumbents seeking reelection has been 88 percent or above for the last twenty years, including in 1994. Over the years too many Republicans could not bring

themselves to eschew the additional fundraising advantages provided by their party's traditional links with Washington's special-
interest lobbies.

This advantage was exploited to the maximum once the
Republicans moved into majority control in 1995. In the first six
months of that year, they not only far surpassed the Democrats in
raising a record $20 million in "soft" money (funds used for the
party's "administrative expenses," not in campaigns), nearly two
fifths of it in checks of $50,000 or more; tobacco company do-
nors led all the rest. They also brazenly warned the major business PACs and their lobbyists to stop contributing money to
Democrats, start contributing more to Republicans, and start ter-
minating the employment of any Democratic lobbyists working
for them.

House Speaker Newt Gingrich, whose own campaign financial
practices have repeatedly been the object of suspicion, declared
(once his party was in power) that more money, not less, should
be spent on politics; that the ceilings on contributions to candidates by their parties and affluent donors should be raised, not
lowered; that the very limited use of public funding to help
equalize presidential campaigns should be abolished, not expanded; and, incidentally, that anyone who disagreed with his
views was engaged in "nonsensical Socialist analysis based on
hatred of the free enterprise system." Earlier moves to enact even
modest reforms in the presently porous campaign finance laws
were blocked for almost two decades as a result of veto threats by
Republican Presidents Reagan and Bush and Republican Senate
filibusters in 1988 and 1994. Lobbying reform was also killed by
a Republican filibuster in 1994 and was repeatedly postponed by
the new Republican leadership in 1995.

Finally, under pressure from the public, from the press, and from Ross Perot, the prospects for at least a tightening of the rules governing lobbyists—and for restrictions on their gifts, free trips, and entertainment for House and Senate members—began to improve late in 1995. (Ironically, the billionaire Texas maverick Perot bought his way into the presidential picture, where he constantly attacks the influence of big money on politics.) More important, the passage of far-reaching federal election campaign finance reforms even in this Congress began to appear possible. For one brief moment in 1995, I was hopeful that agreement could be reached on real reform legislation that included the following:

- Public funding; free or sharply discounted broadcast time (not to be used for commercials either too short to be substantive or in which the candidate does not personally appear and speak), and free or sharply discounted candidate-signed mass mailings. All these would be made available only during a mercifully shortened election campaign period to all nominees, challengers, and incumbents alike, in exchange for their voluntary acceptance of dramatically lowered spending ceilings.
- An outlawing or a deep reduction in the allowable proportion of contributions from PACs and registered lobbyists or anyone other than an individual citizen.
- A strict limit on the sources and amounts of money, hard or soft, that can be contributed to a political party.

Alas, it soon became clear that the Republicans, particularly those in the House, had no serious intention of permitting any serious curbs on PACs or even the continuation, much less the expansion, of public financing. I should have known.

Frankly, I have little confidence that even these relatively extensive reforms would fully or permanently solve the problems they address. Campaign reforms rarely do. Look at the unintended consequences of the Congress's $1,000 contribution limit—it has vastly increased the time spent by candidates to raise funds; the Democratic National Committee's requirement that virtually all Democratic National Convention delegates be selected in statewide primaries or caucuses—it has tilted those enormously more expensive processes in favor of the candidates with the best access to money; and the Supreme Court's decision that campaign expenditures are a form of constitutionally protected free speech—it has spawned a rash of wealthy candidates and unaccountable "independent expenditures" committees. Whatever safeguards surround the electoral process, big money in time finds a way through them. But a start is important. Good intentions are important.

So I am hopeful that the Democratic Party will take a leading role in the enactment of such legislation, and not only because Democrats were wrong to drag their feet on these reforms when they could have passed them, or because they will have a greater need for leveling the campaign finance playing field now that they are in the minority. In my opinion, the Democratic Party's increasing dependence on large contributions from corporate PACs and wealthy individuals over the last fifteen years has regrettably blurred the differences between the parties on special-interest issues, has dimmed the clarity of the Democratic Party's principles, and has diminished the enthusiasm of its constituents. In 1994, Democrats elected to the House received over half their contributed funds from PACs and less than one seventh from small contributions of two hundred dollars or less. Even the

Republicans had a slightly larger base of small contributors than that.

No political genius is required to deduce that many if not most of the high-net-worth donors, business executives, and corporate and trade association PACs who supported the Democrats, almost all of whom contributed to the Republicans as well, fundamentally disagreed with a great many of the basic principles and programs of the Democratic Party. No political genius is required to deduce that those contributions were intended not to advance Democratic principles but to cement a relationship between the donors and key Democratic congressional committee chairmen and members, and thus head off any legislation, investigation, or speeches that, consistent with Democratic Party principles, would be adverse to the donor's interests. No political genius is required, finally, to deduce that the high level of such donations could be maintained only so long as the Democrats, who had become dependent upon them, had a reasonable prospect of maintaining in both Houses the majority control upon which those donors depended. That is a sorry equation for the party of the people.

Who can say how many Democratic voices in Washington against corporate greed or misconduct were stilled, how many legislative proposals were restrained by the natural inclination not to bite the hand that feeds you? One astute observer has noted, "Democrats cannot be the Party of both the little people and big money." No wonder rank-and-file voters, feeling disconnected to and discarded by the whole political process, damned the Democrats and Republicans with equal fervor for becoming the tools of special-interest lobbyists. No wonder that respondents to a poll that asked them to rank in importance those whom the parties represented listed "the rich" first, for Democrats as well as Republicans. No wonder so many lower-income voters who once formed the traditional base of the Democratic Party had too little confidence and too little enthusiasm to go to the polls in November of 1994. It was a long time since Franklin D. Roosevelt publicly attacked the "economic royalists" and declared that "government by organized money is just as dangerous as government by organized mob."

In the end, the withholding from Democratic candidates in this and future years of corporate PAC and other large contributions that once cynically flowed without conviction to the Democratic majority may be a blessing in disguise. Campaign-finance reform that reduces the Democratic Party's dependence on "organized money"—and a massive effort by the Democratic Party to build a broad base of small contributors to replace these PACs and millionaires—will in the long run strengthen the Democratic Party, increase its turnout, and increase its prospects for turning Republican extremism into a Democratic victory.

That will make me very happy—because I am a Democrat.

# ☆ CHAPTER 13 ☆
## RAISING OUR SIGHTS
☆ ☆ ☆

*I am optimistic about the Democratic Party,* because I am optimistic about Americans. As the first year of the Republicans' return to power drew to a close, much of the early talk about permanent realignment had ebbed. The Democrats showed signs of resuscitation, the Republican stampede had slowed, and President Clinton's "job approval" ratings rose. Yet the stark numbers cited in Chapter 12 continued to cast a pall over the Democratic Party's long-term hopes, particularly in the United States Senate. Moreover, though winning a debate, blocking a bad bill, and rising in the polls are all satisfying, they are insufficient. The only way to implement the principles and programs enunciated in the preceding pages and to reverse the destructive path taken by the Gingrich-Dole wrecking crew is for the Democratic Party to become once more the majority party in this country. I firmly believe this can happen.

Even more important than winning another election, the Democratic Party must *deserve* to win and thereby gain not merely a brief interlude between periods of Republican control, not merely a backlash victory as a result of Republican overreaching and self-destruction, but a return to the long-term sustainable public esteem and confidence that the party long enjoyed in the past. In 1996? Perhaps. But "when" is the less important question. The more important question is "how."

My answer to that question takes the form of four broad recommendations that I know are far more easily articulated than implemented:

1. *Conduct clean and constructive campaigns.* Although that is not a radical suggestion, it is totally inconsistent with the belief held by many Democratic campaign experts that Republican dirt must be met with Democratic dirt; that Republican tactics of fear, paranoia, and divisiveness must be countered with Democratic hyperbole, horror stories, and no-holds-barred attacks. It is that kind of cynical tit-for-tat electioneering by both sides that has helped produce a cynical electorate, voters who feel no confidence in the process and no confidence in either party. If Democrats cannot connect their campaign messages to the real lives of enough voters other than political donors and government dependents, they will never reignite the enthusiasm or increase the participation of their own political base.

Making that reconnection will require more than a return to the old days when buttons, bands, bumper stickers, yard signs, and palm cards were much more plentiful in every neighborhood. (I intentionally do not call them the "good old days." Though voter participation in elections—not nominations—was much greater a century ago, so were vote buying, vote stealing, and voter intimidation, as well as unscrutinized, unlimited cash contributions and back-room deals from which women, minorities, and the public in general were excluded.) It will also require more than the new campaign-finance and lobbying-regulation laws urged in previous pages. Indeed, I doubt that new legal codes of any kind will by themselves make our nation's political campaigns worthy of the high democratic principles they should reflect—make them exercises in ideas, not slogans; make them shed light on public issues, not private lives; make them address the national interest, not merely special interests. Such a renewal will require leadership and self-discipline from the parties and politicians themselves. I hope the Democrats will take the first steps.

Let the Democrats be the first to abjure negative campaigning and mean it. For a candidate to criticize an opponent's voting record, proposals, speeches, and campaign techniques is desirable. To question that opponent's character, patriotism, motives, family, or health is reprehensible. In the second half of the twentieth century, the party of Richard Nixon, Joe McCarthy, and Jesse Helms has been especially adept at the use of name-calling, mudslinging, and hate mongering to polarize a campaign and demonize a candidate. Speaker Gingrich has mastered the technique, and his PAC has actively circulated to other Republican candidates a list of words best calculated to smear: "pathetic," "bizarre," "traitorous," "Marxist," "sick," "deviant," "corrupt," and a great many others, to which the Speaker adds "liberal." Not since Franklin and Eleanor Roosevelt has any couple in the White House been subjected to the personally vicious vituperation endured by the Clintons. The urge to fight fire with fire is overwhelming.

But extreme language and tactics befit only an extremist party. Although voter surveys on the efficacy of such attacks are not useful, a few signs are appearing that these tactics may be backfir-

ing. For example, after November 1995's Virginia legislative election, in which the Republicans failed to attain the majority they
had expected, a canny Republican consultant acknowledged that
his party had mistakenly used a "meat ax" instead of a "scalpel."
After the polls and press reported widespread voter complaints
about negative television commercials in this year's first rounds of
Republican caucuses and primaries, the candidates all promised
to "go positive"—a promise they found hard to keep.

Moreover, I wonder whether we ever know the full extent of
the damage done by negative campaigning. Television "attack
commercials," often beginning the year before an election, now
convey insidious images with far more emotional impact and to
far greater audiences than when this sort of malicious misinformation was confined to coffee-shop gossip and local newspaper
circulation. Needless to say, in the typical hit-and-run commercial the candidate who launches the attack rarely if ever voices it
personally.

Let the Democratic candidates be the first to use television as
the political-education tool our nation needs: to convey their own
messages, offering thoughtful, long-term substance instead of
pap, and taking more than fifteen or thirty or even sixty seconds
to challenge their opponents, not to attempt to destroy them. Just
possibly the national network news departments will respond
constructively to this elevation in the national dialogue, by restoring the average daily footage portraying each major nominee on
the evening news to the forty-two seconds or more that once
prevailed instead of today's eight or nine seconds; by promptly
exposing the motives and untruths in any "attack commercials"
that continue to be aired; by seriously analyzing the policies and
proposals of the leading candidates and not merely their progress
in the horse race; and by offering to major party presidential

nominees, in addition to full-length debates against one another, a free weekly hour or a nightly five minutes in the two months before Election Day for that nominee's personal appearance and use in educating, not manipulating, public opinion on the real issues.

A principled Democratic campaign—making no promises that cannot be delivered, offering no "solutions" not likely to succeed, proposing no programs without revealing their cost, evading no issue, however controversial, and appealing to the voters' intelligence and sense of responsibility and not merely their self-interests—may only be a dream. Indeed, it would probably be a nightmare for professional political consultants who are accustomed to doing whatever it takes to win, emphasizing tactics over beliefs, fundraising over values, and the importance of sound bites, photo ops, and spin over ideas and issues. They want their candidates to base their speeches on focus groups, poll responses, and market-tested phrases, not on their own convictions. Such consultants will likely suggest to candidates who favor such voluntary reforms that they simply keep a "deniable" distance from the dirt. Campaign advisers will likely regard such reforms as, well, "nice." They will not like them. But I think the voters will.

2. *Reunite behind a new coalition of concerned citizens, not a collection of interest groups.* The Republicans have done us a favor, not only by sending us a wake-up call in the 1994 elections, but by pressing upon the nation a cutback and rollback program so harsh and extreme that Democrats of every stripe and shape, noted for their disunity, can now unite against that program. The departure from our party of conservative Southerners who have consistently voted against the party's programs and principles makes that unity still easier. A political struggle for nothing less than the kind of society our children will inherit—one bitterly

divided along lines of wealth, race, religion, and locale versus one joined in pursuit of an expanding economy characterized by both opportunity and fairness—makes that unity essential and petty factionalism unconscionable.

Somehow, even in our traditionally broad-based, undisciplined, unruly party, we must strive to achieve the same commitment to common objectives, the same solidarity and sense of purpose, that Mr. Gingrich and his conservative Republicans have achieved; we must unite not merely behind the party name and candidates, not merely in opposition to our adversary, but in support of the basic themes and principles that distinguish our party from our opponents.

Democrats in and out of elective office who publicly complained last year about the Democratic President's leadership, or publicly urged him to bow out, or privately advised him to distance himself from the party's principles or from its congressional members, or to show his independence by denouncing some long-term Democratic support base, were only fueling voter suspicions that the Democrats are too disorganized and disingenuous to be entrusted with governing again. Democratic candidates whose strategy today is to reach Republican donors by turning their backs on long-term Democratic supporters—for example, faithful Democrats who are actively seeking to preserve the environment, or economic equity, or civil rights, or the rights of women, workers, and the disabled—are mistaken if they believe that those voters will remain Democrats because they "have no other place to go," however much they are ignored or taken for granted. They do have some other place to go. They can go home, and stay home, and some have.

But party unity that is forced and not felt, or based merely on opposition not conviction, on personalities not principles, will not long endure. Unity requires work, patience, and discipline. It does not require unanimity in all details—fortunately, inasmuch as no broad-based party such as ours could achieve absolute agreement on anything. On the contrary, leaders of a revived Democratic Party must no longer be afraid to speak out for fear of offending some powerful constituent group, right-wing religious network, generous corporate donor, or even some small bloc of congressional Democrats. They should no longer be equivocal or evasive on controversial issues on which any clear-cut position will alienate one or another group of voters or contributors. They should no longer hold their fire on inequitable Republican programs for fear of being charged with "favoring a redistribution of wealth," "fomenting class warfare," or even being "liberal." They should not be afraid to stand up and expose Willy Horton–type smear commercials, or to stand up to the intimidation tactics of the gun lobby and antiabortion pressure groups.

Let the Republicans fight among themselves on the "cultural and religious" issues about which they are so passionate, while the Democrats foster unity by focusing on the major economic and social issues that are far more relevant to the daily lives of ordinary people: wages, job security and retirement, health and child care, education, and all the rest. So long as Democrats control the White House, it should now be possible for executive branch and congressional Democrats to forge a common legislative program and budget, each respecting the other's constitutional role. It should now be possible for self-identified New Democrats, New Deal Democrats—all Democrats—to agree on measures to help all Americans who need help, whether hungry or ill or headed for college or held back by discrimination, and to agree as well on a list of basic principles that distinguish virtually all Democrats from the Republican right.

It should be possible now for Democratic factions created by past events, like Vietnam or NAFTA, to unite on future legislation and leadership, on goals that unify the party, on policies that do not set black against white or city against suburb or Eastern states against Western but instead have the broadest possible appeal and application to all Americans. It should be possible now for all active Democrats to reach out together to those who identify with neither political party and are skeptical of both, skeptical of politics and government and the establishment in general. For they are the voters who now hold the balance of power in their hands and are likely to decide at least the next several elections.

Most important, Democrats must avoid policies and political practices that divide or castigate either the poor or the middle class, or set them against each other. Simply put, most people in this country work for someone else, or are trying to do so, or once did so before they were laid off or retired. Whether their collar is white, pink, blue, or otherwise, and whatever their race, education, union status, or position on the economic ladder, most of them today are concerned about their position on that ladder, striving to climb up, fearful of sliding down. Logically, all of them, poor and middle class alike, should be united by the principles of the Democratic Party, not divided by the politics of the Republican Party. But the latter, which has never demonstrated much interest in the poor, even the working poor, has in recent years made successful inroads into middle-class households by falsely portraying the Democratic Party as the party that represents only welfare mothers, racial minorities, and higher taxes.

The Democratic Party, as a matter of moral obligation as well as conviction, cannot and need not turn its back upon the truly disadvantaged of all races and ages, those long adrift in rural areas and inner cities and those newly arrived on our shores, those who are employed, unemployed, or underemployed, and those who are educated, uneducated, or undereducated. But neither can the Democratic Party afford to lose touch with or lose respect for the middle-income families who still constitute the great bulk of the electorate, the economic backbone of the country, and the traditional base of the Democratic Party. (Note: This assumes, of course, a different definition of "middle-class" than that recently offered by a Republican Congressman from North Carolina: "someone who is making anywhere from $300,000 to $750,000." I am not making this up.)

Most members of the true middle class today are frustrated, hard-pressed, often embittered by decades without any effective after inflation increases in compensation and benefits, and they have not seen the Democratic Party doing much about those problems in Washington. They hear union leaders blame free trade, and Republican leaders blame affirmative action, and they watch as Democratic leaders both solicit more campaign funds from the very corporate bosses who are squeezing them and distribute more public funds to the poor and minority workers who could undercut them.

The Democratic Party has both a responsibility and an opportunity to unite the poor and middle class, as Roosevelt did in the thirties and as the Progressive movement did a generation or more earlier. For it is the Democratic Party's programs and proposals for education—from Head Start to college loans to job training and retraining and all the rest—that are the key to both the middle class's survival in our changing economy and the prospects of the poor trying to climb out of poverty. The Republicans oppose them.

It is the Democratic Party's programs and proposals for health care—from Medicare to Medicaid to portable and comprehensive insurance—that address the single largest cost concern of both the middle class and the poor. The Republicans oppose them. The list is long: Democratic programs and proposals on housing, retirement income, park and seashore preservation, community development, and other measures providing economic opportunity and fairness for both those struggling to stay in the middle class and those striving to join it. The Republicans oppose them.

It would be tempting for the Democratic Party to begin this process of reuniting its voters by turning for help first and foremost to sympathetic Washington interest groups that have the necessary staff, membership lists, and money. Many highly admirable, constructive public policy organizations, labor unions, consumer groups, and others share a common view with the Democratic Party, on issues ranging from the environment to civil rights and from health care to child care. I do not lump those advocacy organizations with such Republican handmaidens as the National Rifle Association and the Christian Coalition. But I hope the Democratic Party's new appeal for votes can be based not merely on voter self-interest but on the national interest. It must voice that appeal to individual citizens and local Democratic gatherings, not through PACs and pressure groups, and it must rebuild the party at the grass-roots level, creating a large base of small donors instead of relying so extensively on a small base of large donors.

Politics in this country, with the help of pollsters as well as pressure groups, has gone too far down the road of viewing voters in categories of self-interest. I have attempted to indicate that, regardless of the "categories" with which I might be identified, my choice of political party is based upon my own moral roots and core values, developed as I grew up in Nebraska. I

believe many if not most Americans make up their minds that
way—not necessarily or solely as farmers or veterans or white
male retirees but as Americans, with common concerns and beliefs and obligations that transcend those categorical lines. No
group is monolithic, no vote is totally predictable. For example,
surveys show that a substantial number of born-again Christian
women vote Democratic and a substantial number of gay businessmen vote Republican. The electorate does not vote as blocs,
groups, and organizations. People vote as individuals.

Unfortunately, the Democratic Party, like the Republican, has
become too dependent upon organizations that purport to represent the blocs, interests, and attitudes sympathetic to the Democratic philosophy (to say nothing of its dependence for funds on
those who are in fact unsympathetic to its philosophy). I know
from personal experience that even the national Democratic Party
platform comes under continual pressure from business, ethnic,
single-issue, and similar organizations who insist upon the inclusion of their pet proposals and key buzzwords, however unmean-
ingful those phrases may be to the general rank and file of the
party. That is a good example of why most individual voters feel
left out. They have no lobbyist or PAC, and even the issue organizations that they admire do not always speak for them.

The Democratic Party, in short, must build from the bottom
up a national party of citizens in place of its present coalition of
special interest groups and blocs. Those organizations, after all,
fall in and out of favor as their agendas and leaders change. No
matter how well-meaning, friendly, or helpful those groups may
be today, a party dependent upon such a coalition would be
unable to control its own destiny or to form a coherent national
vision. Moreover, as the astute Al From of the Democratic Leadership Conference has observed, issue politics, as distinguished

from interest group politics, plays to the strengths of the Democratic Party.

3. *Sharply define our differences with the Republicans.* The Democratic Party's principal problem in 1994–95 was not, as often claimed, a "communications problem," a failure to get its message out and understood. It was not a tactical problem or a marketing problem or an image problem. The party has no shortage of brilliant political communicators, tacticians, marketers, and image makers, as well as speechwriters, slogan artists, television packagers, advertising consultants, and other "handlers." No, the party's principal problem has been its continuing lack of a clearly defined and consistently agreed-upon position on most of the major issues facing the country today. Particularly in 1995, the party, its leaders, its members, and the general public could not be certain where it stood or where it was headed, what it intended to fight for, not simply whom it intended to fight against. No amount of tactical and marketing skills can—or should— overcome this fundamental deficiency.

To fill this void, several options are available. The first is for the Democratic Party to be all things to all people, shifting position with each opinion poll, political breeze, and audience. But a party that tries to please every voter ultimately pleases few and deserves none. Leaders make choices, and choices cost votes.

A second option is to adopt all or most of the Republican Party's major positions—for example, rejecting any national commitment to the poor, emasculating educational and environmental programs, placing the cost of health care out of reach to many elderly, and increasing military spending far beyond any discernible need. That strategy would make the Democratic Party seemingly invulnerable to Republican attack—also irrelevant, superfluous, and unlikely to retain even its most loyal supporters.

A third option is to be just a little less Republican than the
Republicans, to compromise away the issues by agreeing to most
but not quite all of their rollbacks, to cut just a little less, to
dismantle a bit more slowly. Genuine compromise is often a
practical and responsible necessity to keep our system function-
ing or to salvage the shred of a cherished program. But compromise that does permanent damage to human lives is
unacceptable; compromise with fanatics on principles like religious liberty or racial justice is immoral; and compromise for the
purpose of obscuring fundamental differences of principle is dishonest—and will never get the right-wing ideologues out of
Washington.

A fourth option is to attack Republican solutions without providing any of our own. Action limited to exposing and combating
Republican positions is better than none, but it is inadequate. No
successful party can define itself solely by what it is against—just
as it cannot succeed by ignoring the other party's positions and
stating only what it favors.

Some Democratic members of Congress and some presidential
advisers clearly considered one or more of all these options last
year. But ultimately, the only feasible and successful option for
the Democratic Party is the fifth and best: to spell out clearly
where and how its affirmative positions differ from those of the
Republicans. The Republicans have made this task easier for us:
First, Speaker Gingrich and his crew have forthrightly focused his
party on basic issues of governance and policy, a contest that an
issues-oriented party like the Democrats should prefer to compe-
titions in personality, mudslinging, or campaign spending. Second, Mr. Gingrich's team has carried its right-wing rollback
revolution to such extremes that much of the electorate, including Republican moderates, is alarmed. Those who joined the

party of Abraham Lincoln, Teddy Roosevelt, Robert La Follete, Jacob Javits, Clifford Case, John Sherman Cooper, and Nelson Rockefeller cannot be comfortable today with a party increasingly committed, with dwindling room for dissenters, to the very ideologies their heroes fought. In this context, defining and declaring the major issues that divide the two parties becomes not merely the Democratic Party's obligation but an immense political opportunity as well.

I hope this book can make a modest contribution to that articulation of basic differences—not our differences on specific bills, dates, or sums but on basic principles. The box that follows lists some of those differences discussed in the preceding pages.

---

## BASIC PARTY POSITIONS

Most Democratic, unlike most Republican, office-holders believe the following:

- *Public or Private Interests*   Government should serve the public interest, which is paramount, and not simply get out of the way of private interests, which the Republicans believe are paramount.
- *Government or Market Rule*   The federal government, kept lean and honest and staffed by honorable and dedicated public servants, can help solve major national problems, such as health-care access and environmental preservation, that are created or aggravated by an unregulated market.

- *Job Security* The federal government, through better education, job training and retraining, minimum wages, and other reforms, must address the stagnation and decline of real wages and benefits, the failure of workers to receive their share of productivity gains, the growing gap between the rich and the rest of America, and the increasingly desperate condition of the poor.
- *Equal Opportunity* Civil rights guarantees, including affirmative action in education and employment, are necessary to help assure equal opportunity to all of our citizens and make the fullest use of their talents, regardless of race or gender.
- *National Leadership* The devolution of more program authority and administration to state and local governments, and to private citizens and entities, can be achieved without the splintering of uniform national standards and national policy-making leadership among fifty state governments ill equipped or unwilling to meet politically unpopular national obligations.
- *Fiscal Fairness* A policy of savaging social insurance and education programs and shredding the national safety net (while not cutting "corporate welfare," local pork, redundant military projects, or tax loopholes for the rich) as the primary means of reversing the Reagan-Bush budget deficits is not fair to the young, the poor, the elderly, the unskilled, or the infirm, nor is it necessary.
- *Law and Order* True law and order require attacking not only crime but also its causes, and enhancing—not weakening—gun control, equal access to the courts, and respect for the Constitution.
- *Family Integrity and Privacy* Strengthening family values

requires strengthening the family's economic opportunity, not compromising the separation of church and state or the rights of privacy and choice in personal lives.

- *World Leadership*   To maintain its leadership in the post–Cold War world, America must honor its international obligations, participate in multilateral organizations, and reject protectionism, unilateralism, and fiscal isolationism.

- *Little People*   Government must give priority to the needs of ordinary citizens, workers, consumers, students, children, the elderly and the ill, the vulnerable and the underdog, and not to the needs of those already sufficiently powerful and affluent to afford their own lobbyists.

In one sense, this boxed summary overstates the split between the parties by omitting the many items, mentioned in earlier chapters, on which the parties are in basic agreement—on the need for keeping America strong and at peace, for example, and for fiscal discipline and restraint.

But in another sense, the table fails to convey adequately just how far to the right, away from the political mainstream, the Republicans have been pushed by their ascendant conservative wing: the hardhearted, short-sighted, and dogmatic insistence of the Republican right on dismantling environmental protection, collective security, and the safety net, for example, and the Republican Party's prevailing attitude of exclusion, even scorn, for those whom it believes do not measure up to its moral and material standards. In contrast, the actual positions of the Democrats, so often exaggerated by Republican cries that we are captives of the left, turn out to be quite moderate and sensible.

Republican positions should also be compared with the basic

principles of their own "revolution." After successfully exploiting voter fears that government under the Democrats was too cozy with the special interests, too large and intrusive, and not to be trusted, recall that the Republican Party, upon taking majority control of the Congress, produced a legislative program and budget that primarily benefited the special interests, deliberately intruded into the private lives and prayers of ordinary citizens, reneged on term limits and other commitments, and was certain to increase the very economic frustration and anger that their campaign's "revolutionary" rhetoric so successfully exploited.

I realize that some Democrats, who win term after term by emphasizing constituent errands and bipartisan compromises instead of defending partisan positions, regard this sharpening of the differences between the two parties as a risk. I regard it as a necessity.

4. *Become once again the Party of New Ideas and the Party of Conscience.* Defining ourselves in terms of our differences with the opposition—on the basis of both their reaction to old Democratic programs and our reaction to new Republican proposals—is important, but it is not enough. It is too easy: today's Republicans are extremists. It is too ephemeral: tomorrow's Republicans might not be extremists. It is too passive: Democrats can win but cannot rule on the basis of what they are not. It is too incoherent: a scattershot of complaints, rejoinders, and attacks do not constitute an agenda or even a platform, much less a governing philosophy—and certainly not a vision that either lasts or looks beyond the next evening's newscast.

Once the Democratic Party was the party of new ideas—the progressive party, the party of hope and change, the trail-blazing party, the party that took initiatives and risks. Not only new ideas but big ideas—Social Security, reciprocal trade, the United Nations, the Marshall Plan, civil rights, space travel to the moon. But for many years, in part because of divided government and fiscal pressures, Democrats in Washington have talked mostly—not exclusively but mostly—of small-scale proposals, timid new steps, minor adjustments, and tactical responses to the Republican opposition.

In a new age where old ideas and programs no longer suffice and the public is increasingly skeptical about government's role, the Democrats must and can become once again the party of change and effective new ideas. More than reinvention, the Democratic Party requires a renewal of its former courage and vision. The public's trust will be renewed only if the party clearly presents a coherent package of realistic proposals for change consistent with its ideals and goals, then fights for those proposals with conviction and consistency until they are adopted, then implements them efficiently and openly, and accepts the public's verdict on their success or failure. That public trust will be further heightened if the party is willing to revisit, restructure, and even replace existing programs that, though traditionally valued, may be no more suitable to the challenges of today's Information Age than the nineteenth-century Agricultural Age's programs were suited to fight an Industrial Age depression in the 1930s.

If such a new legislative package is to consist of more than superficial campaign devices, it may take years of study and development; thus, the time to begin is now, without waiting for majority control of both houses of Congress and the White House.

The area on which to focus, in my view, is not the budget-reducing, tax-reducing, government-reducing area staked out by the Republicans, though our positions in this area must be made clear. Nor should the focus be on the highly divisive social and cultural issues pushed by the religious right, though our resistance to those incursions must be unflagging. Instead, the focus of a new Democratic legislative package should be on the most basic issue confronting most Americans today: their jobs, income, and security. Their principal concern is not balancing the federal government's budget but balancing their own family budgets; not the greater redistribution of federal power to the states but the greater redistribution of corporate earnings to the workers; not which Medicare bill should pass first but which medical bill their families must pay first. They know that ideology can affect their lives in the long run, but insecurity afflicts their lives now.

The persistent lag in worker compensation and benefits will not be easily reversed. The old pattern of large industries bargaining with large labor unions has largely disappeared. The lack of college-level scientific, technological, engineering, and other skills needed for the expanding computerized and intellectualized enterprises of tomorrow is not quickly overcome. The diminished need of the private sector for low-skill and no-skill workers is permanent. Broad fiscal, monetary, and economic policies, no matter how successful in terms of national statistics, no longer lift all the boats.

Nevertheless, we must begin by raising our sights economically as well as politically. Last winter's Republican budget negotiators projected that their programs would produce a growth rate in the American economy of 2.3 percent, and they assailed President Clinton's projection of 2.5 percent as unrealistically high and risky. They blocked the nomination of Felix Rohatyn to the Federal Reserve Board because he favored even greater growth. Yet, prior to the Reagan years, this country had long enjoyed annual growth rates consistently exceeding 3 percent in real dollars. More well-paid workers in more good jobs can help restore that higher rate of growth, and vice versa.

In addition to expanding instead of shrinking the nation's investment in public education and student loans, we need to develop coordinated programs of (1) job generation at all levels for those who are qualified and (2) job training and retraining for those who are not. This year is the fiftieth anniversary of the enactment of the Employment Act of 1946. In that law the federal government committed itself to maximizing the availability of jobs for all American workers. That effort, already watered down when enacted, has now languished. But the act's basic thrust and commitments could be revitalized in a new law, this time working primarily through contracts with private employers who could be paid a profitable success fee for providing training and jobs at a lower cost (per family rescued) than either welfare or prison.

State and city governments, labor unions, community colleges, and nonprofit institutions could also play a role without adding to the Washington bureaucracy. Experts should examine the feasibility of creating specially earmarked or dedicated funds for these programs, comparable to those used to finance America's network of interstate highways; they should examine as well the possibility of distributing "opportunity vouchers" for training and jobs in place of cash.

I am not smart enough to know how best to structure and implement such a concept. But I do know that more permanent and better-paying private-sector jobs can relieve much of the anxiety unsettling our nation. I also know that more public-sector and nonprofit employment would be useful to rebuild and replace our crumbling and outmoded infrastructure (transportation, affordable housing, educational facilities, waste and water treatment plants, parks and playgrounds and day care centers) and would provide more trained health- and child-care personnel, whose work would enable more women to be employed elsewhere. I do know that training and education will be key, and Washington Democrats should find out more about innovative successes in such programs at the state, local, and private-sector level. Incidentally, giving the private sector a profit incentive to help achieve these public interest goals is neither new nor contrary to the philosophy of the Democratic Party.

Finally, however, the party to be trusted by the American people is the party that has not only a program but a soul, that has unshakable core convictions about what policy is right and wrong for the people of America, not merely what is popular and clever. Historically, the Democratic Party has been the "party of conscience" in America. It has shown more compassion for ordinary people, more concern for workers and consumers, and more consideration for the middle class and poor, despite the preponderance of influence and money on the other side of the street. It has led the battle against discrimination, segregation, and prejudice based on race and color, despite the certainty of alienating a substantial portion of the party's oldest base in the Deep South. It underwent a cathartic but wrenching debate on morality versus expediency over the war in Vietnam, despite warnings from union leaders and others that staunchly Democratic members who were hawks were leaving the party in disgust. President Clinton has led the fight for NAFTA, GATT, loans to Mexico, affirmative action, and American participation in peacekeeping in Bosnia, despite groundswells of dissent in the ranks of likely Democratic supporters.

In countless other instances, Democrats have had the courage to put principle ahead of politics: Wilson and the League of Nations, Johnson and the War on Poverty, Carter and the Panama Canal treaties. In each case, the national interest was upheld, the party's interests suffered.

But in recent years, except for the Clinton actions noted, too many Democratic officeholders have seemed more interested in political contributions than political courage, in holding on by going along with whatever course was easy or popular, in appealing only to the voters' personal pocketbooks and not also to their national pride and responsibility. These Democrats, I regret to say, learned to play special-interest politics almost as well as the Republicans, to accede to each new request for federal funds, to back away from the party's traditional concern for those most subject to deprivation or discrimination, and to join with the Republicans in delaying the reform of campaign finance and lobbying laws. Relatively little that was bold and new was offered to address the concerns of those most adversely affected by the economic trends of the new era.

This vacuum of moral courage must be filled, and there is no likelihood of the Republicans' filling it. Alabama's George Wallace was wrong in his 1968 third-party slogan that there was "not a dime's worth of difference" between the two major parties, and that slogan is still wrong today. The difference is more than a dime and more important than dollars. It is a difference in values, a difference between Republicans who have consistently rejected change and Democrats who have consistently welcomed it, between Republicans who fashioned a Contract With America out of polls and Democrats who stand up for what is right, regardless of polls, between a Republican Party built on self-interest and fear and a Democratic Party built on progress and hope.

Clearly, of the two major parties today, only the Democratic

Party has the history, philosophy, diversity, and constituency to become once again the Party of Conscience, to challenge once again the special interests—indeed, to challenge the American people to meet their own individual and community obligations. Only the Democratic Party can restore public confidence in our political system and lead a now cynical and dispirited electorate back to a renaissance of the democratic (and Democratic) standard.

Throughout its history, the Democratic Party has produced national leaders whose greatness met the nation's needs. Not all became President. Witness Al Smith and Adlai Stevenson. Not all were honored for their greatness while they served as President. Witness Harry Truman. Not all were recognized as presidential material a year or more before their nomination. For their greatness stemmed not so much from their personalities as from the principles they enunciated and implemented—the fundamental principles of the Democratic Party.

That is why I am optimistic that the Democratic Party will continue to produce such national leaders in the twenty-first century: leaders prepared to address the inequities and uncertainties that Republican scapegoating, moralizing, and benefit cutting can never resolve; leaders whose greatness of purpose and heart can attract countless men and women, yearning for a positive vision of action, to the ranks of the Democratic Party and to the call of public service. I know from my own years in public service on behalf of a caring and committed Democratic leader that there is no greater satisfaction. Serving the paramount public interest, serving "the better angels of our nature," is what the Democratic Party, and its fight with Republicanism, is all about.

Why, then, have I even raised these doubts, complaints, and regrets about the recent timidity of the party I support, no doubt displeasing its leaders and displeasing my friends in that party, especially in a book devoted to setting forth why I am a Democrat? Because, like most Democrats, I am open to change in the party but not to changing parties. Because I want to win, and because I believe a broad-based, wide-open Democratic Party will be more likely to win against an increasingly narrow-minded, narrowly based Republican Party—*if* the Democrats are willing to display the kind of conscience, courage, and compassion that has made our party great in the past. Because I want Democratic politics once again to illuminate our national condition and extend our national horizon and inspire our national vision. Because I want the Democrats to lead an America that is not only militarily, diplomatically, economically, and intellectually strong but morally strong as well. Because I want Democratic politics as well as policies to offer hope once again to those who have given up on our system, while renewing all that is best in that system.

Hope and renewal. That is what the Democratic Party offers. That is why I am a Democrat.

# ☆ INDEX ☆